Josep Lluís Mateo

ON BUILDING

Matter and Form

Contents

On Building is an action that moves towards the future. It involves imagining another reality, another world, different to this one.
The project requires data about existing conditions: the place and its rumours, the use and its references, matter and its conventions. Yet the project distorts this data (and must do so): the place will (and must) be irremissibly changed, the use will evolve, it cannot be easily frozen, pacified, domesticated. The project will also distort the matter or, even better, give it meaning: stone will be glass, or *vice versa*. The project will always reinvent, at least partially, the technology it employs.
The project as a necessary moment of invention looks to the future.

Building is a long journey through the present continuous. The past exists as an echo, as a phantasmal form that is no longer discussed, and sometimes even its origin is forgotten.
Building means taking root in the mud, squelching through it on a journey without distant horizons. We get used to short, sometimes microscopic distances. The present, detained and expanded, sometimes seems eternal, a place where I, at least, prefer to abandon any hope of transcendence.

Finally, the building appears. Despite the slowness of construction, suddenly, the building is there. It is as though sustained effort over a long period of time is the initiatory condition that brings about its sudden appearance. And so we see it: whole, new, young, brilliant. Very soon, we will leave it.

This book describes that initial moment of a series of buildings, beyond their origins and their physical constitution (both issues, idea and matter, however, based on my work).
Here, the objects are presented, captured by Adrià Goula, as visual forms, as compositions of planes and surfaces that form volumes and also as a dialectic of the light and shade that define spaces. Set among the images, like axe blows in the mass, are words and, at the end, the principles of order determined by the plans.

The idea, however, is to convey the initial, fresh force of the objects when they appear. Witnessing these brief moments is, in part, what motivates our work.

Josep Lluís Mateo

The history and the setting of the building also have to be taken into account. In this case, we were looking at the former Renault plant, which immediately brought to mind old stories of May 1968 and Jean-Luc Godard's film *Éloge de l'amour* that was made there shortly before the factory was demolished. However, when we visited the site, what we found was a huge, beautiful, expectant empty space, which involved constructing a new part of the city. As an architect, I like that sensation of emptiness waiting to be filled and taking on the responsibility of imposing clarity.

However, this is a building designed in terms of volume and thickness, not just of skin. The façades are structural concrete walls, which were a major technological challenge, but the kind of challenge a true constructor loves. The proportion and size of the openings were calculated in relation to the structural behaviour of the building. For reasons of energy consumption, the walls, which I would have liked to leave bare, called for thick thermal insulation, which we then protected with aluminium sheeting. The side walls that continue the roof are of zinc, a traditional artisan material that has a great urban tradition.

Josep Lluís Mateo

Text from an oral explanation

53

FACTORY

STRUCTURE

Agustí Obiol

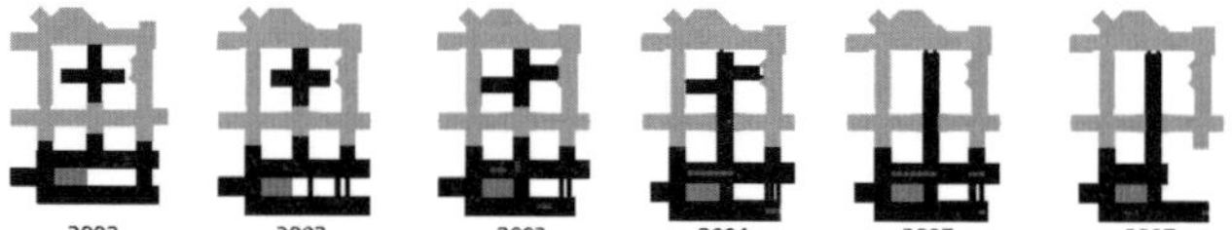

2002 2003 2003 2004 2007 2007

Ideas are fast, construction is slow.
The planimetric layout was very clear from the start: to the continuous form of the old building a new figure was counterposed, made up of lines that interrelated without bending (like the sticks in the Japanese game of Mikado). This gave way to a figure, which, while similar to the old building, was much more open. This figure was frequently varied for multiple reasons, particularly of an economic nature.
It was like a pattern that could easily evolve, be reduced and extended, without changing in quality.

Josep Lluís Mateo

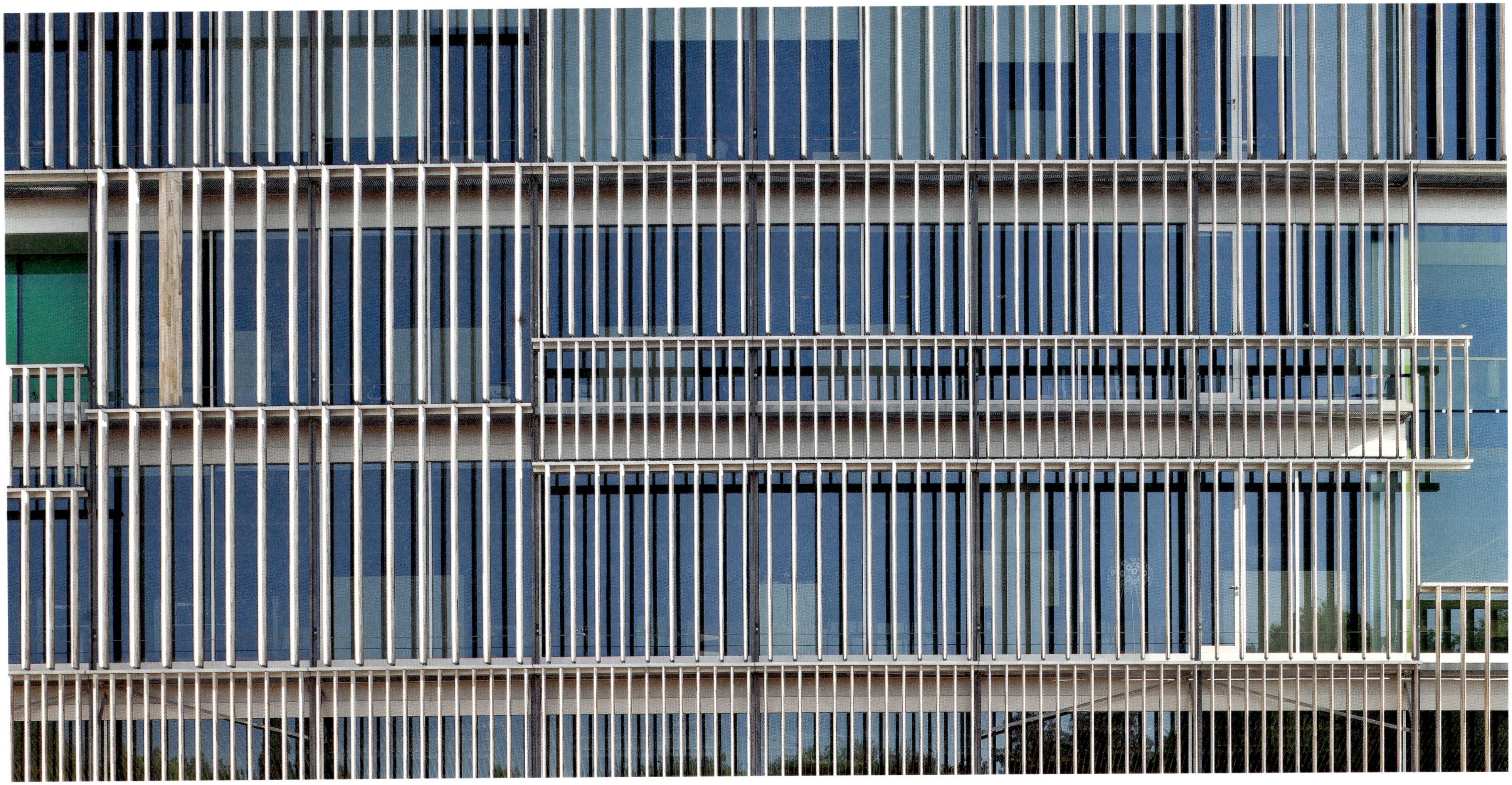

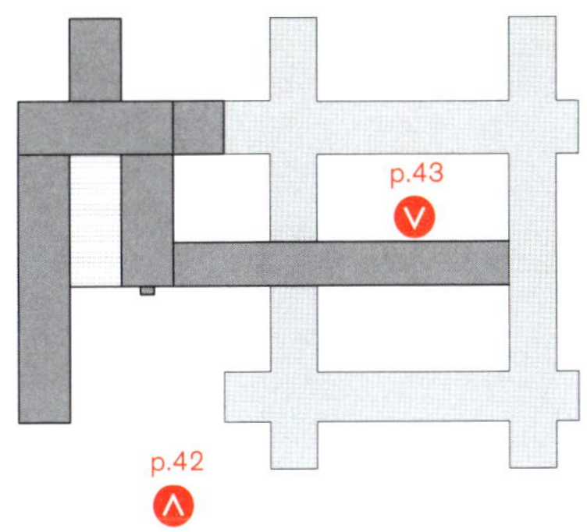

p.43
p.42

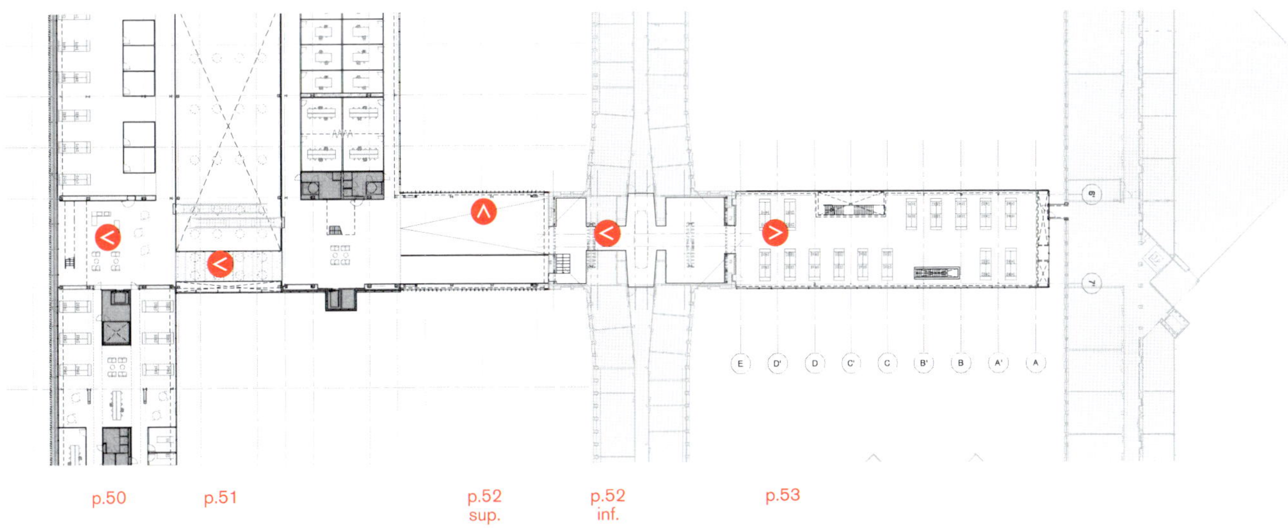

E
D'
D
C'
C
B'
B
A'
A
p.50
p.51
p.52
sup.
p.52
inf.
p.53

DEPTH

Dominique Boudet

On various occasions, we were asked to intervene in the most public areas of a lovely building dating from the 1950s (the work of the architect Francesc Mitjans).
The entrance hall had been disfigured by a series of interventions that had rendered it complex and disjointed; we set out to clarify its function and its urban role.
The interiors are communicated by a circular staircase, which we freely restored. The floor slopes gradually to change level in order to avoid the existing steps, and the ceiling constantly reacts to these movements.
The ceiling, particularly in the innermost areas, serves to concentrate the light and is highly expressive.

Josep Lluís Mateo

Sabadell Atlántico

BancoUrquijo

Sabadell Atlántico

Sabadell Atlántico

BancoUrquijo

Bloqueig Targeta
BSMòbil
caixa
caixa

3.5120; ELE; 19.9400; ENG

caixa
caixa
caixa

caixa

The retaining wall to the rear that anchors the house to the hillside was
extremely lovely. As well as expressing the effort of retaining the earth,
it concentrated in one place the oven and the point of collection of
the water that filters through it.
Earth, water, fire.
The entire intervention gravitates around it.
The rest is white, untainted, abstract. The preceding trilogy is joined by air.

Josep Lluís Mateo

RESISTANCE

Fredy Massad and Alicia Guerrero

About the form

The ruins mark the structure of the buildings. The Roman forum formalizes the floor plan of foundations and drains.

In the old town, my building sets out to express itself as pure structure—no cladding, no finishes.

The bare concrete beams-cum-walls form the façades that, in their diversity, prove themselves members of the family of the dilapidated neighbouring walls, where plaster crumbles to reveal their original central mass.

Filters are juxtaposed on the wall. This cinematographic metaphor is not just conceptual; it is above all physical, sensible. In the old town, with very close relations between buildings, interaction must be mediated, filtered. And this is implemented by a variety of devices, with a vague cinematographic reference.

About the space

The space is organized around two movements:

a) The descent into the darkness of the cinemas, with the reflection of the spectators (in turn reflected, actors seen in a series of mirrors).

b) The ascent towards the light, towards the places of work.

Two courtyards, connected but not continuous, accompany and construct the movement.

Josep Lluís Mateo

FilmoTeca
de Catalunya

GSM RED

Time
CD, DVD
VCD
VIDEO CLUB

MATTER AND MEMORY

Philip Ursprung

Architectural photography is a task of searching. Buildings implicitly contain, in their geometry, the potential viewpoints that the photographer must know how to find. It is, then, a question of investigating, of tracing, of discovering.

Built spaces contain a series of axes and alignments that emerge from the design process, remains of lines on the plans drawn by the architect. Part of the photographer's task is knowing how to recognise them, how to feel them, and, having identified them, to adapt to them. Positioning himself where the building tells him. As though it were not so much a question of offering a personal viewpoint—a look—but an image that emanates from the object and is the consequence of its way of being, its way of manifesting itself. The photographer does not choose the viewpoint; the work dictates it. When the correct position has been found and the right lighting conditions occur, the order contained in the work of architecture structures the image, too. If the proportions, the symmetries and the alignments are transferred from the work of architecture to the photograph, a parallel is created between these two worlds, giving rise to something that goes beyond the image. Not only does the building appear, its very essence surfaces, allowing us to see the architecture by means of the photograph —it allows the photograph to *re-present* the architecture.

Like the performer who has to discover the composer's intentions in order to explore all the possibilities and opportunities contained in the piece of music, the architectural photographer has to find the potential of the work of architecture. He has to analyse, study, try to perceive the architect's purpose if he is ultimately to create the version of the original piece that manages to express its essence. Producing a good photograph depends not only on himself, then, but on coming face to face with an inspiring work containing nuances and complexities that allow him gradually to discover it.

The work of Josep Lluís Mateo offers this opportunity. Juxtapositions and clearly outlined limits run the building through with precision from top to bottom. Spaces, structures and volumes are forcefully shown. Visual permeabilities and the landscape seem to establish unexpected relations. Everything corresponds to design decisions that are manifested without contradiction in the work. An internal coherence where all the elements are precisely interrelated and generate a formal unity that offers constant photo opportunities.

I like to think that the images in this book constitute the last step in the long history of a series of projects in which many people have been professionally and personally involved. It is the judicious completion of all of these processes of conceptualization, design and construction that informs these photographs—images that, ultimately, contain the complexity of simply producing architecture.

Adrià Goula

First prize. Invited Competition. 3 phases
2006-2010. Paris/France

Location: Rue Émile Zola, Boulogne-Billancourt, Paris
Surface: 15,500 m^2
Client: VINCI Immobilier d'entreprise / NEXITY Entreprises

External collaborators
Structure and installations: SNC Lavalin / Agustí Obiol-BOMA
Quality control: VERITAS
Fire protection: EURO Coord
Energy control: COTEBA Environnement
Acoustics: Lasa
Landscaping: D'ici-là
Façades: Interface
Constructor: Sicra

LOCATION

When addressing this project for an office building, we started off by thinking about the entire city block as a series of buildings with spaces between them to introduce light and air into the empty space. In this way we began to see the building as a mass that formed Rue Émile Zola, like a complex volume. We had some prior experience with this type of building in terms of dimensions, depth, and so on, that went almost automatically into the drawings and models. I always start this way, with a very abstract volume as a base.

The history and the setting of the building also have to be taken into account. In this case, we were looking at the former Renault plant, which immediately brought to mind old stories of May 1968 and Jean-Luc Godard's film *Éloge de l'amour* that was made there shortly before the factory was demolished. However, when we visited the site, what we found was a huge, beautiful, expectant empty space, which involved constructing a new part of the city. As an architect, I like that sensation of emptiness waiting to be filled and taking on the responsibility of imposing clarity.

The main constraints of the site were the street, the inner courtyard and the adjacent elements. The site's relation with the street suggested that the building should fold to protect the pavement in a very striking urban gesture: you move alongside the building and, at the same time, beneath it. It is a contemporary version of the old porches. The building provides refuge, protects you and then gently lets you go as you pass. It also opens up on the ground floor, connecting you with the garden at its centre which, though not big, is very lovely. The top line of the building is not horizontal; it slopes, adapting to the different heights of its neighbours and increasing the dynamism of the vanishing point.

Evidently, the programme too presented constraints, producing some singular results. It called for flexible generic office space that will adapt to future users, but we also created particular spaces, such as the entrance, restaurant, conference rooms and foyers, which I hope will make it special. This type of project calls for clarity and regularity, to which we have, I hope, brought a new complexity. For example, seeing the façade made up of a constellation of different windows sets off an attractive many-faceted vibration in the interior.

However, this is a building designed in terms of volume and thickness, not just of skin. The façades are structural concrete walls, which were a major technological challenge, but the kind of challenge a true constructor loves. The proportion and size of the openings were calculated in relation to the structural behaviour of the building. For reasons of energy consumption, the walls, which I would have liked to leave bare, called for thick thermal insulation, which we then protected with aluminium sheeting. The side walls that continue the roof are of zinc, a traditional artisan material that has a great urban tradition.

Another important factor is the project's response to HQE, France's high-quality environmental standards to manage environmental impact. The building has great thermal inertia, as it is well insulated and hermetic. In the south side, the windows are drawn back for protection from the sun, offering views of the established trees in the garden. The mechanical installations incorporate all the latest advances, and the design integrates them rather than merely attaching them to the building. This is particularly striking in the roof, where the slope of the building is used to accommodate all the machinery. Technology is present but invisible.

Josep Lluís Mateo
Text from an oral explanation

COMPETITION MODEL OF THE STREET BLOCK

MODEL OF THE MAIN FAÇADE, WITH A SMALL ANNEXED BUILDING

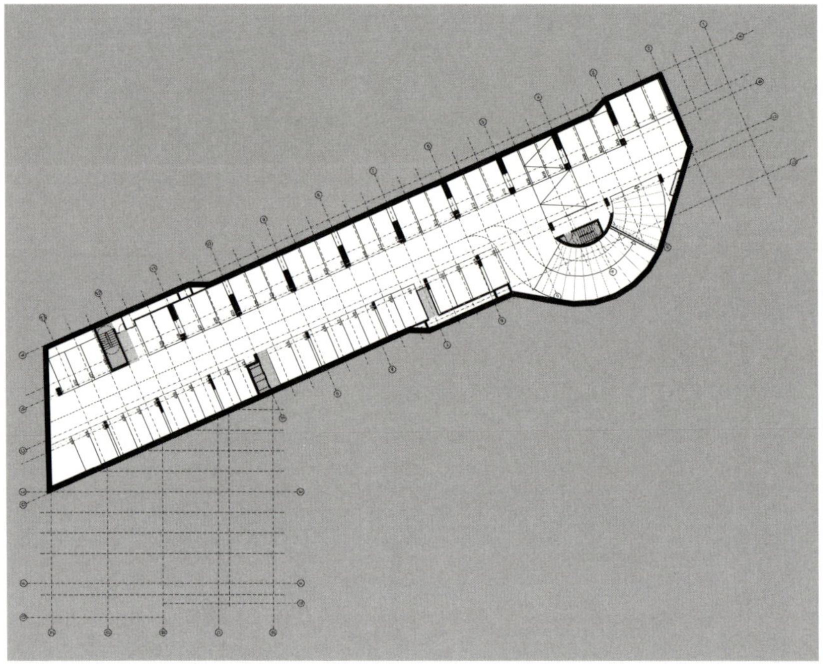

BASEMENT 2 FLOOR PLAN

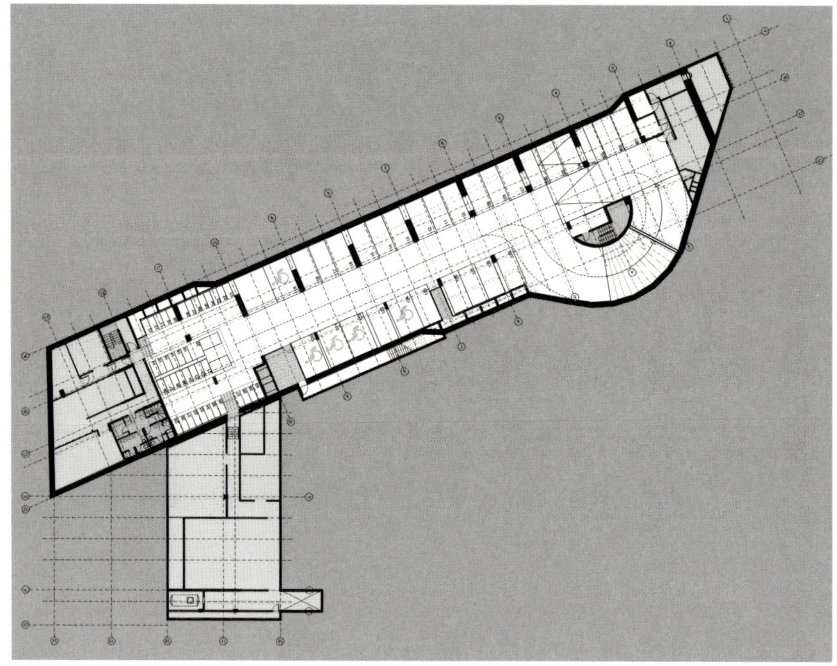

BASEMENT 1 FLOOR PLAN

MODEL OF THE GARDEN, BY D'ICI-LÀ, LANDSCAPING

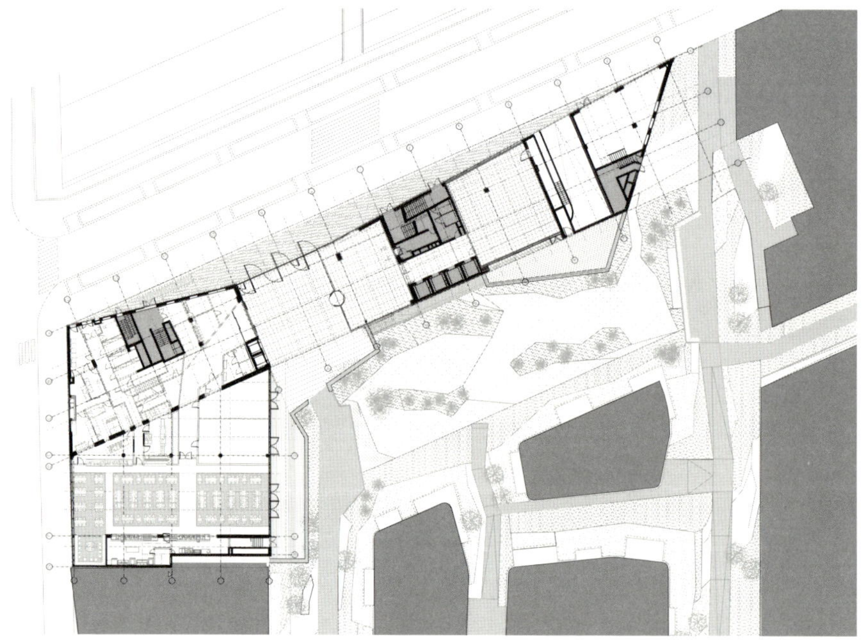

GROUND FLOOR PLAN

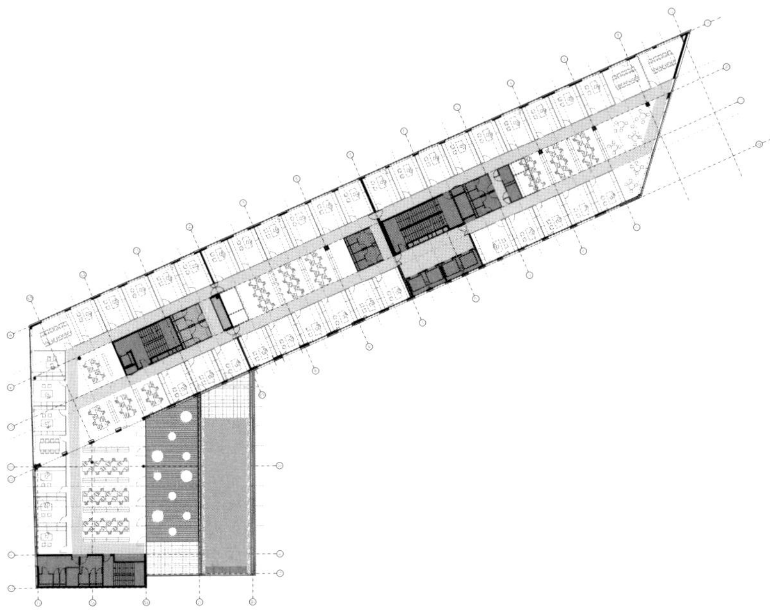

FIRST FLOOR PLAN

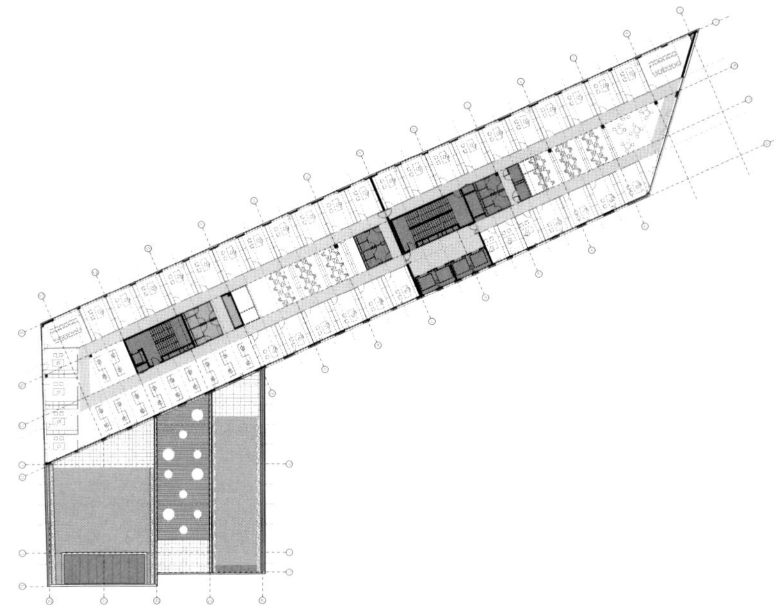

THIRD FLOOR PLAN

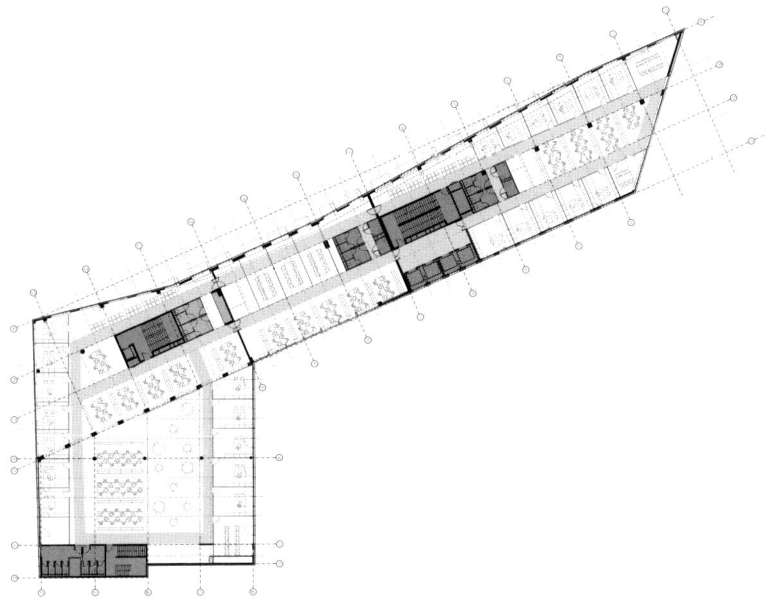

FIFTH FLOOR PLAN

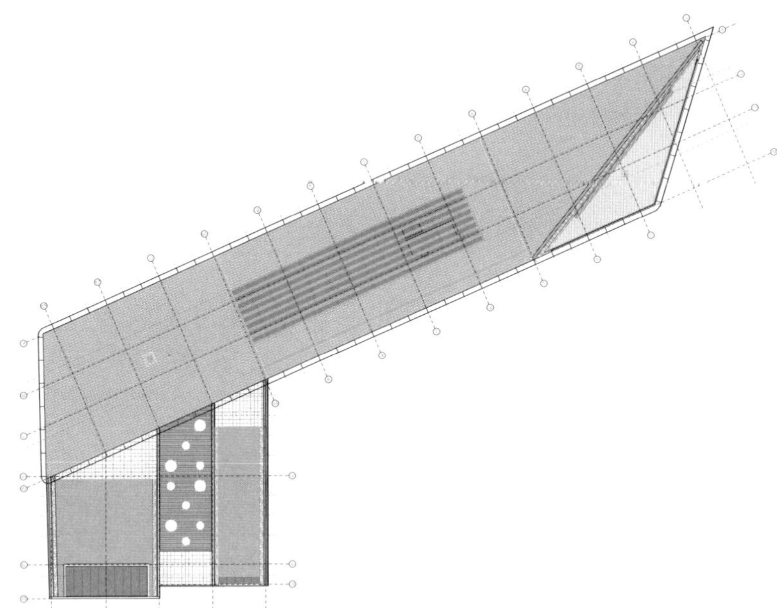

NINTH FLOOR PLAN

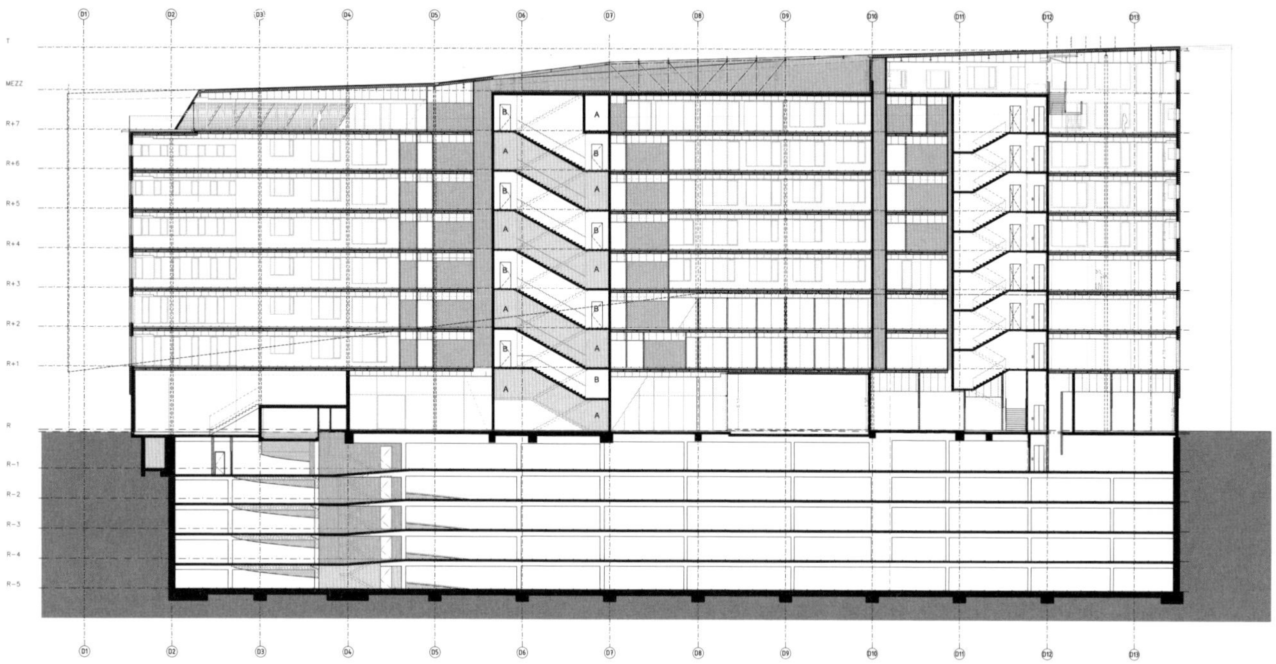

LONGITUDINAL SECTION

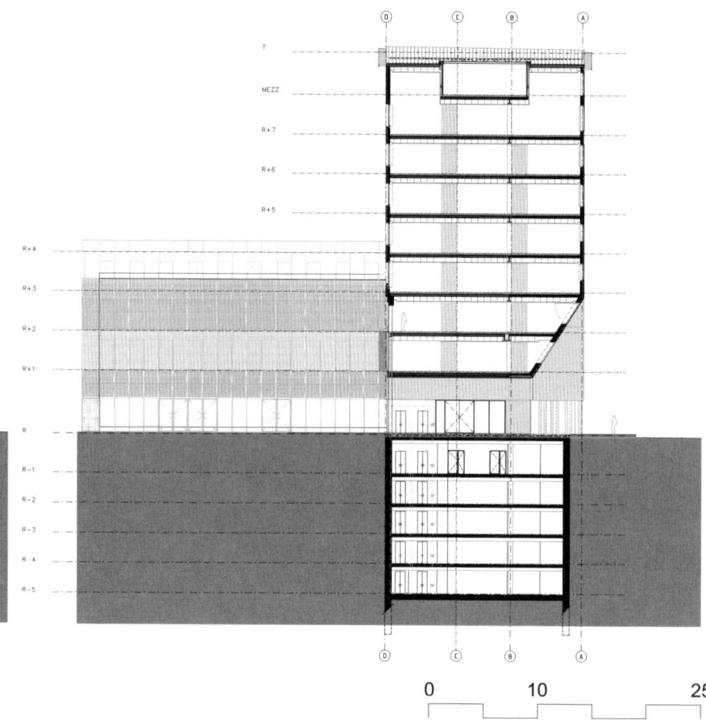

CROSS SECTION

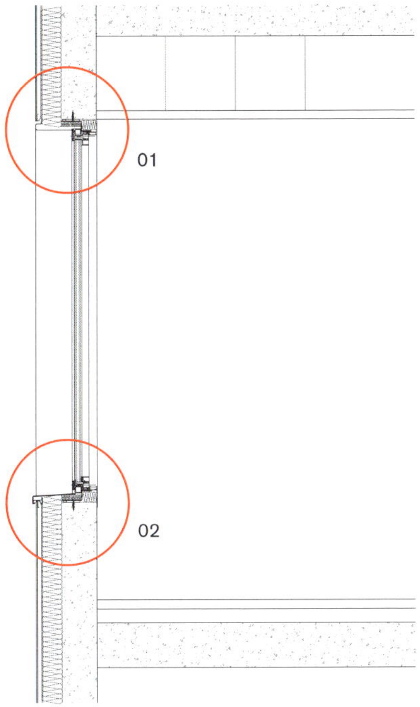

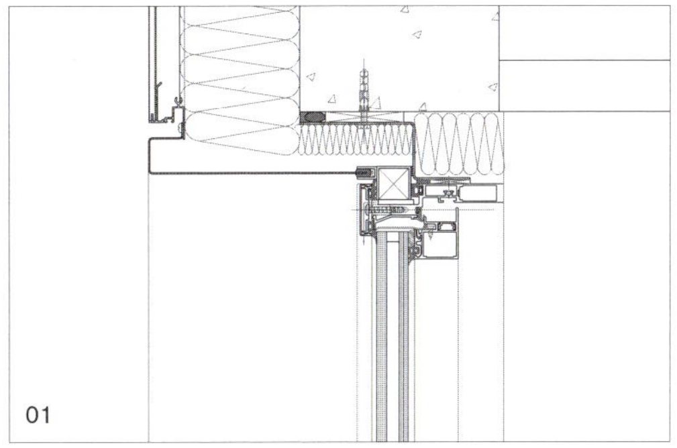

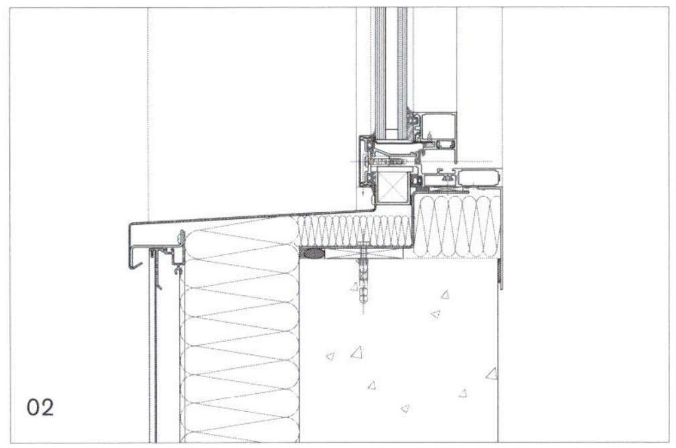

DETAIL OF WINDOWS IN SOUTH FAÇADE

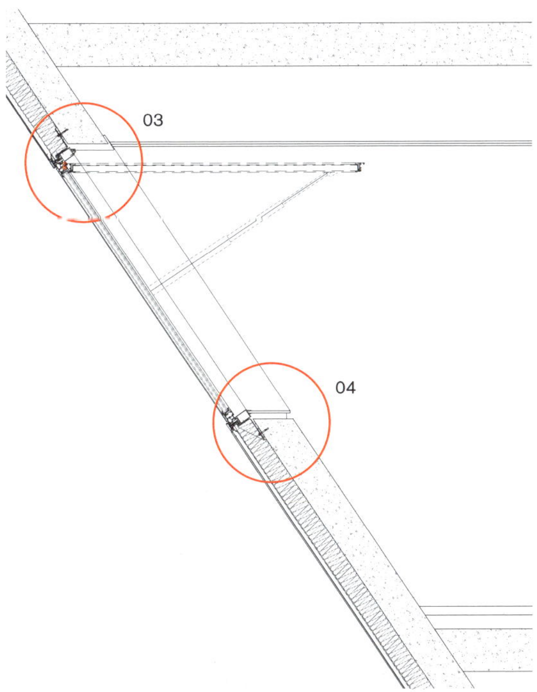

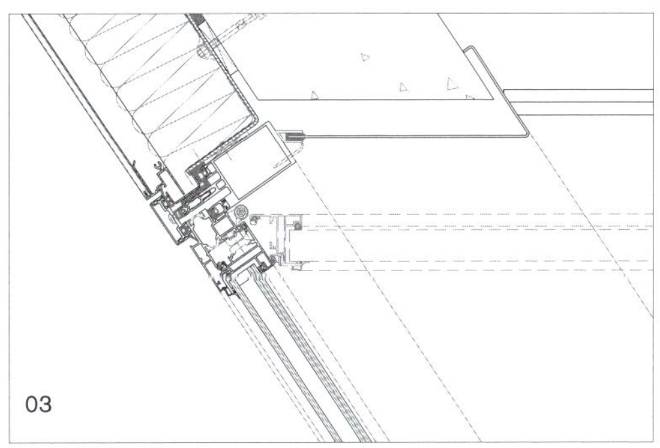

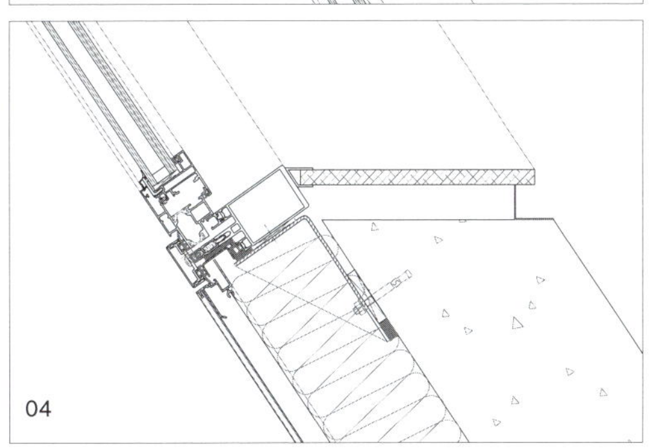

DETAIL OF WINDOWS IN NORTH FAÇADE

PGGM COMPANY HEADQUARTERS ZEIST, NETHERLANDS 2011

First Prize. Invited competition
2002-2011. Zeist, Netherlands

Location: Noordweg Noord, Zeist
Surface: 25,000 m² offices, 25,000 m² parking spaces
Client: PGGM Insurance Company

External collaborators
Structures: Zonnefeld
Installations: Deerns
Landscaping: Deltavorm
Local architect: ADP-Marc a Campo
Contractor: Ballast Nedam

LOCATION. PREVIOUS STATE

Josep Lluís Mateo
MAP Architects

Teodor Roviralta 39
E08022 Barcelona

T + 34 932 186 358
F + 34 932 185 292

map@maparchitect.com
www.mateo-maparchitect.com

With regard to the question in hand, two issues interested me:
- Firstly, how to expand the existing building, making it twice its current size, and
- Secondly, how to address the landscape.

At this very basic level, our ideas are to:
1. Work at the scale of the old building
2. Continue your suggestion: densifying the court (with an independent structural element) and constructing the new building in front of the existing one. We have come up with several possibilities and envisage a clear structural connection with the underground level.
3. Use greenery as a continuous layer, with the new buildings floating above it into the landscape.

We are interested in conceptual architecture but also in its precise materialization.

Josep Lluis Mateo

LETTER FROM JOSEP LLUÍS MATEO TO THE CLIENT. START OF THE PROJECT

LOCATION. BUILDING EXTENSION (COMPETITION)

COMPETITION MODEL

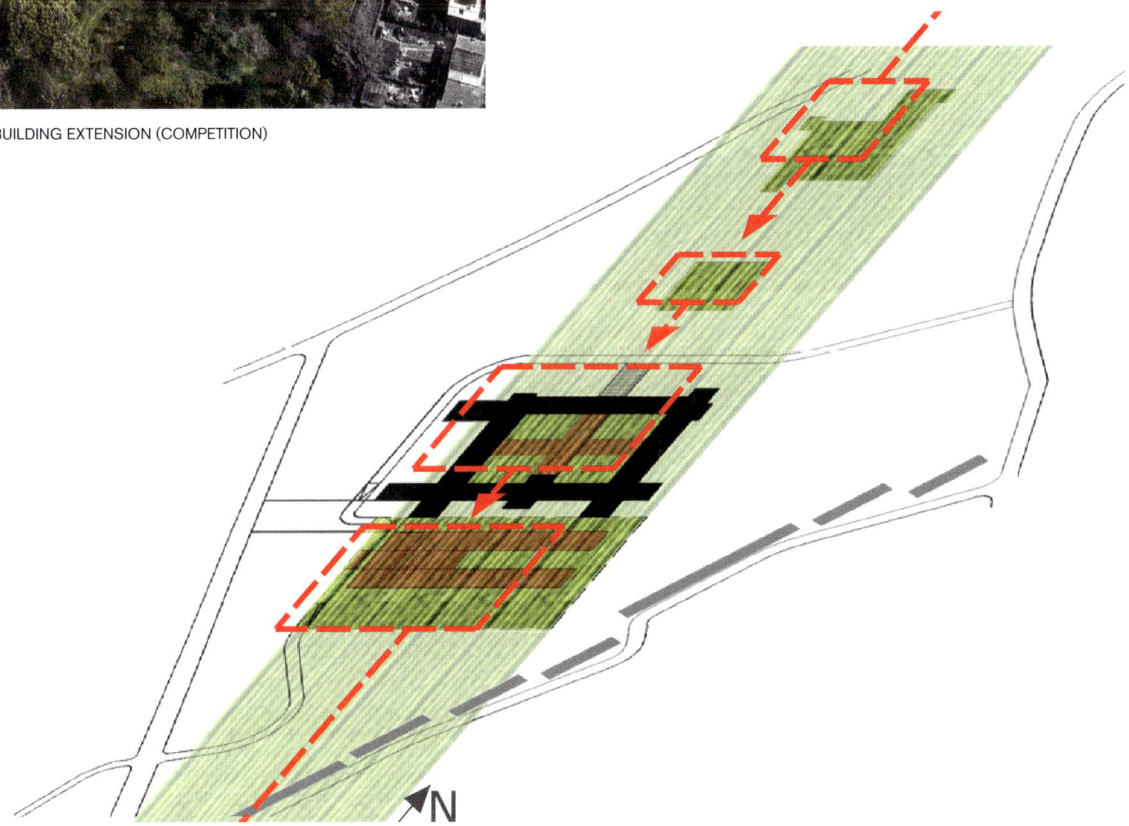

DIAGRAM OF THE SEQUENCE OF CLOISTER BUILDINGS (COMPETITION)

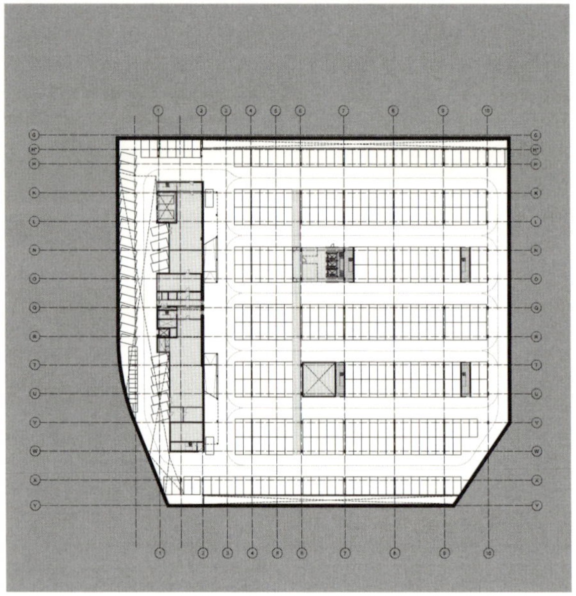

BASEMENT 3 FLOOR PLAN

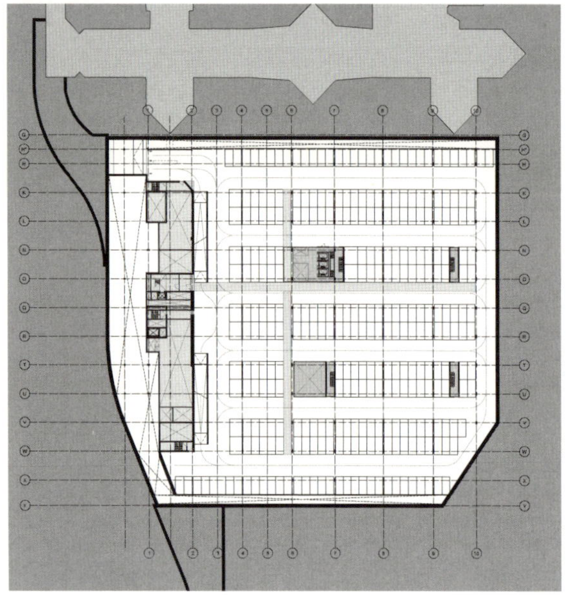

BASEMENT 2 FLOOR PLAN

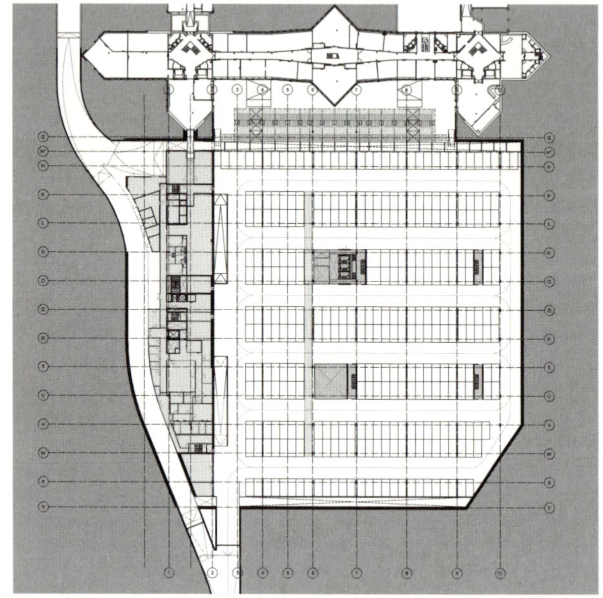

BASEMENT 1 FLOOR PLAN

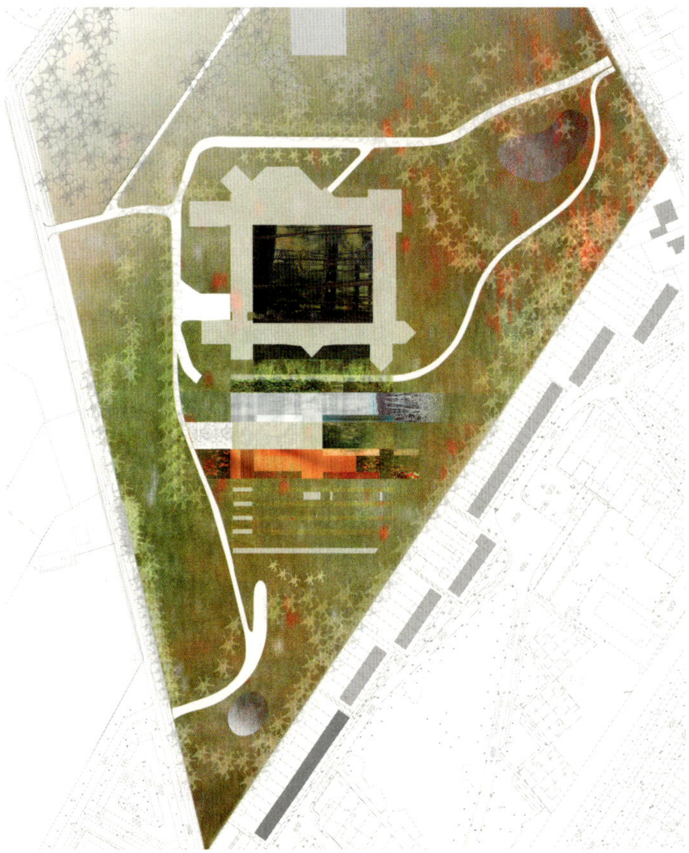

LOCATION

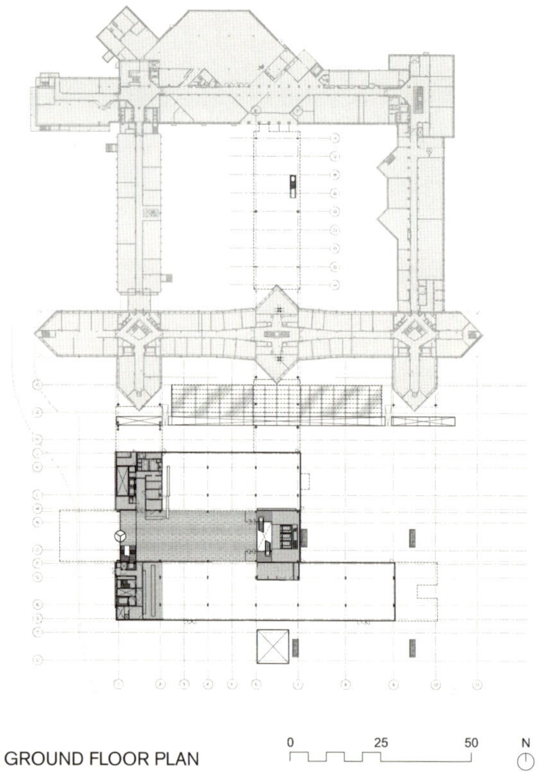

GROUND FLOOR PLAN

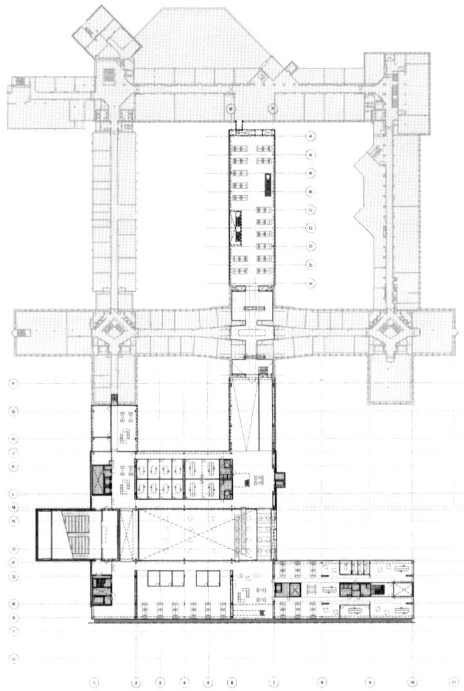

FIRST FLOOR PLAN

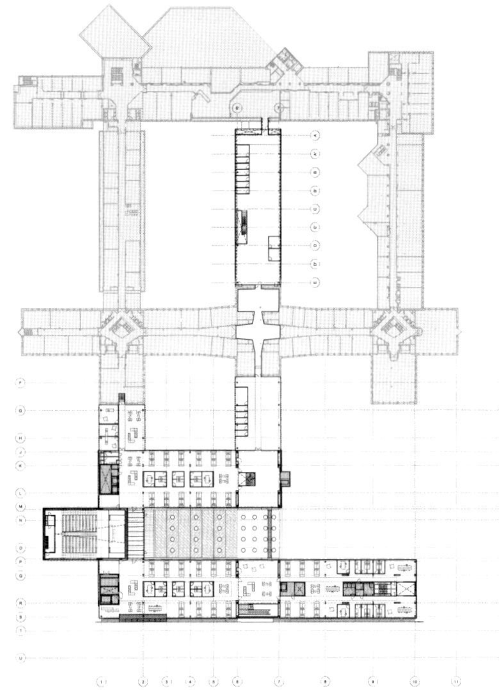

SECOND FLOOR PLAN

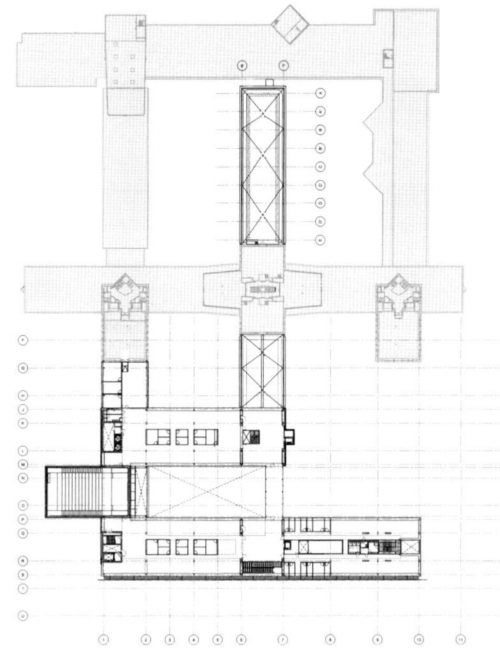

THIRD FLOOR PLAN

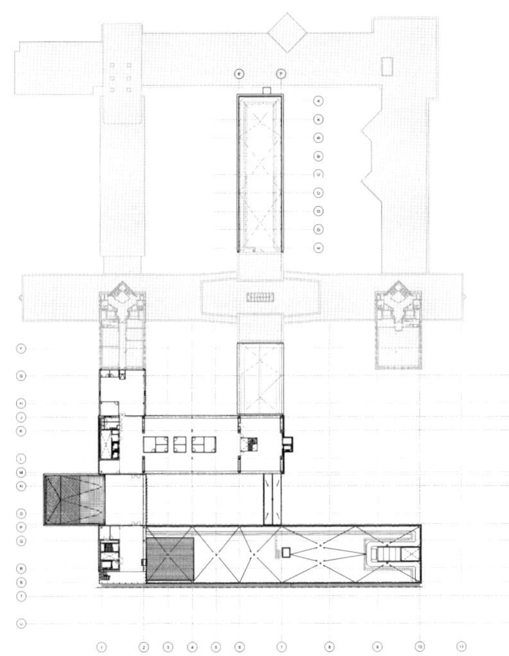

FOURTH FLOOR PLAN

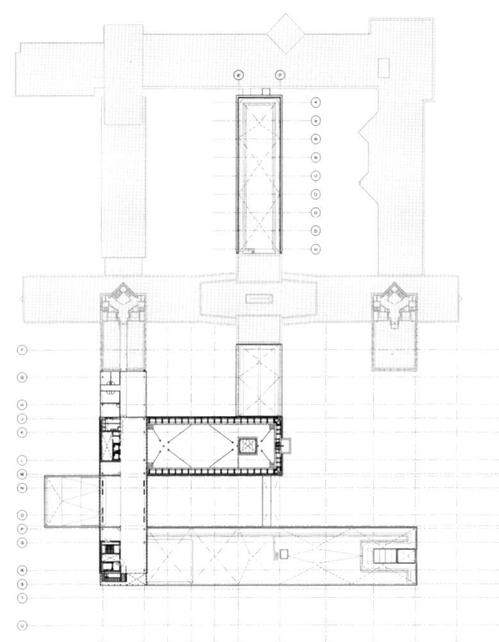

FIFTH FLOOR PLAN

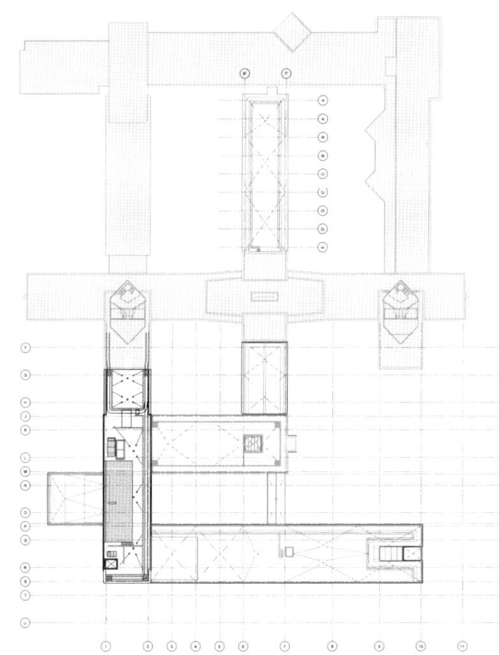

SIXTH FLOOR PLAN

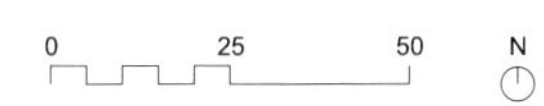

The installations

The installations in the new head offices of PGGM in Zeist are developed according to sustainable criteria. The design will result in a use of energy at least 20% lower than government requirements. The cooling and heating for the climate installation will be provided by aquifer thermal energy storage (ATES).
ATES means that, during the warm season, water from the cold store at around 7-10°C passes through a heat exchanger to provide direct cooling water to the building. The heat pump is available automatically as support in periods of peak demand.
The store circuit water collects energy from the building, increasing in temperature to around 18-20°C (or higher for fresh air load). This water, higher in temperature than the natural groundwater, is run to an underground warm energy store.
The contents of the warm energy store are used for heating in winter. Water from the store at around 20°C is passed through a heat exchanger and connected to a heat pump, which in turn provides water at around 40-50°C to heat the building. As the groundwater passes through the heat pump it cools to around 7°C and is then run to the underground cold energy store.
The cold energy store is used for cooling, completing the annual cycle. Any excess heat or cold in the system over a year is balanced out using an external heat exchanger.
In the building, the cold and warm water runs through climate ceilings. In this way, during most of the summer cooling is provided directly by groundwater, a free form of cooling.

The ventilation system is based on overpressure. This means the air is distributed by ducts and leaves the building through specially designed valves in the façade. Air ducts and ventilators are not needed for the return air. Instead of recovering heat from return air with a conventional heat wheel, the heat from the cooling system collected during the summer is used for pre-heating the fresh air in the winter. The heat is stored in the ATES system.

Lucien Engels (Deerns Raadgevende Ingenieurs Bv)

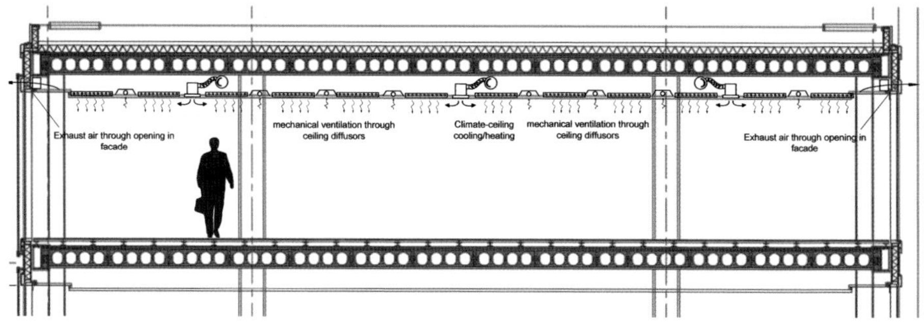

TYPICAL SECTION : OFFICES

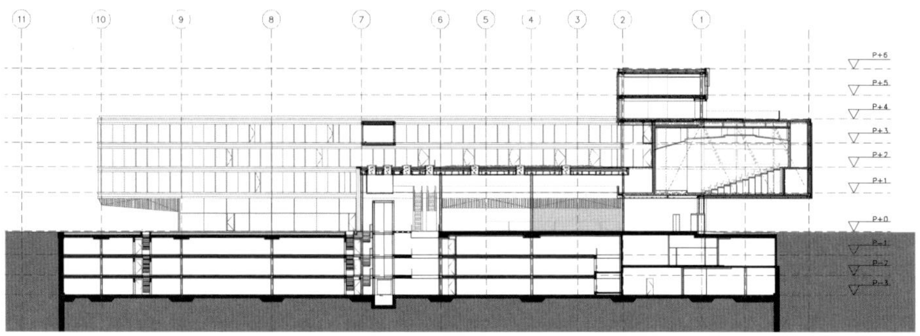

CROSS SECTION

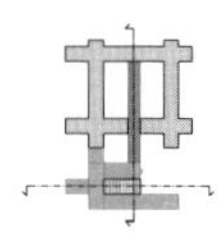

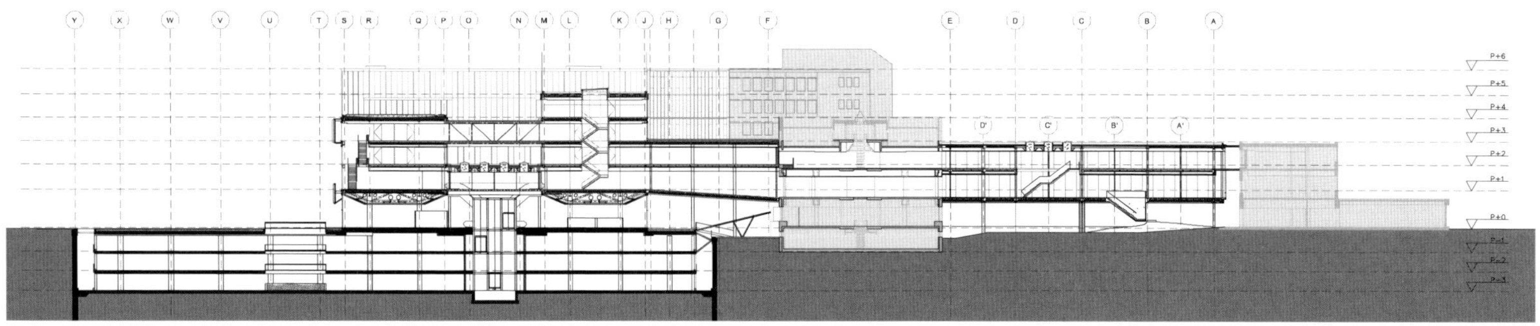

LONGITUDINAL SECTION

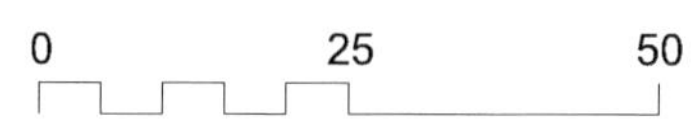

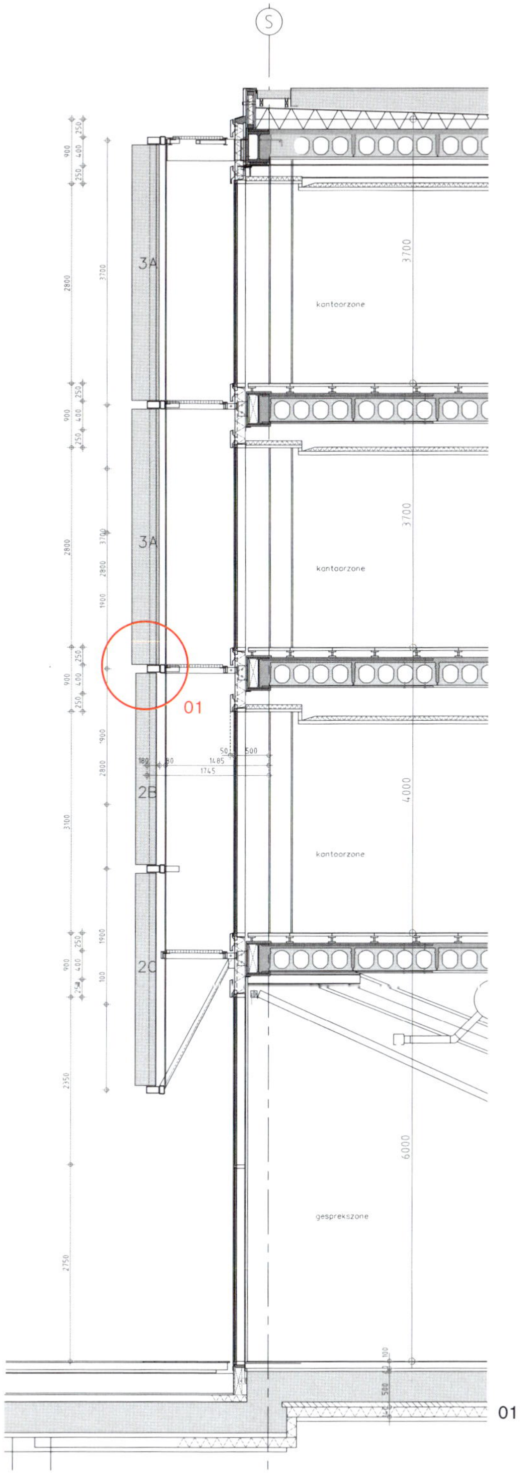

SECTION OF THE FAÇADE WITH WOODEN SLATS

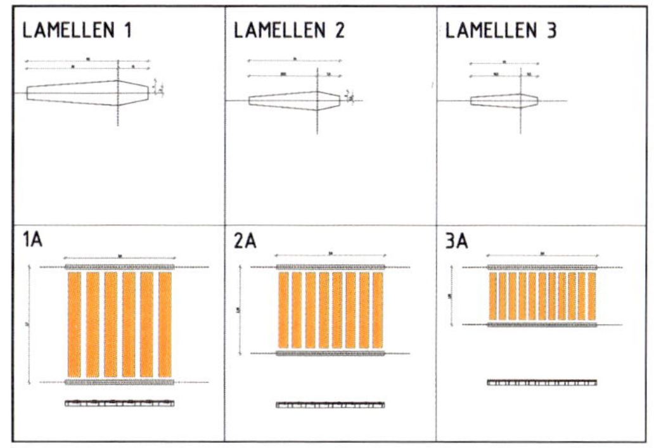

BREAKDOWN OF THE SLATS

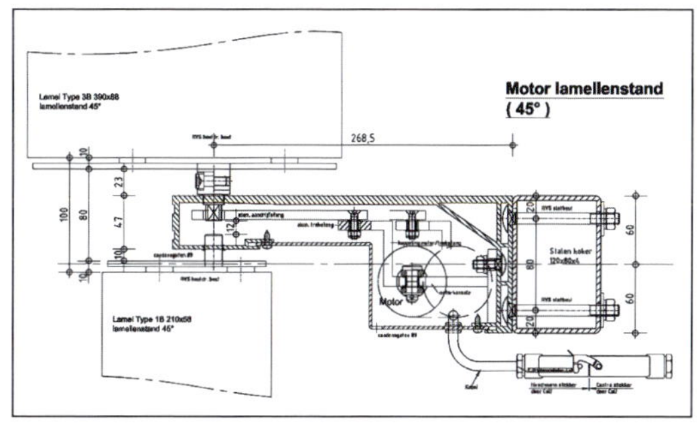

01: DETAIL OF THE JOINT BETWEEN SLATS

PROTOTYPE OF SLATS

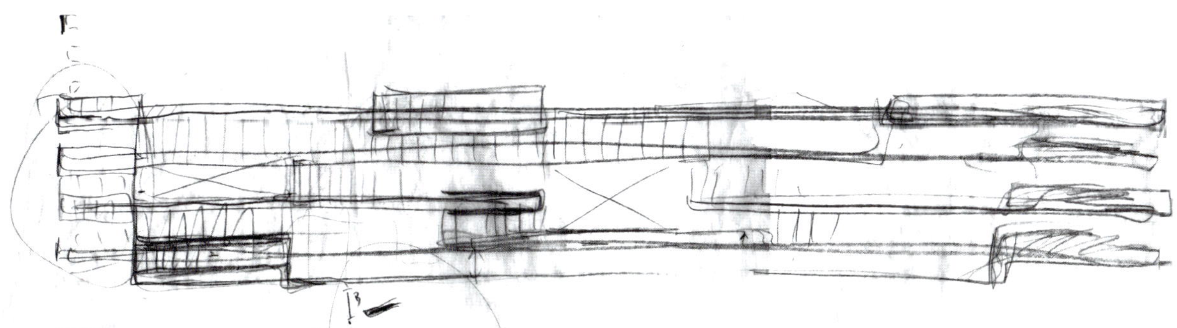

SKETCH

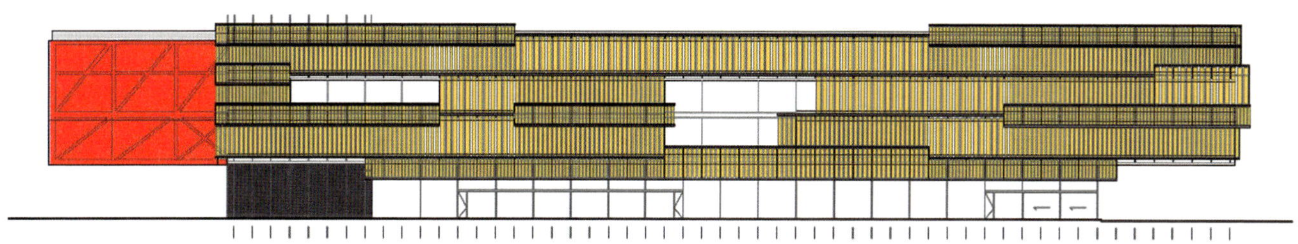

ELEVATION OF THE FAÇADE WITH WOODEN SLATS

2006-2010. Barcelona

Location: Avinguda Diagonal with Balmes, Barcelona
Surface: 1,000 m^2
Client: Banc Sabadell

External collaborators:
Structure: BOMA
Technical architect: Francina Bernad (Banc Sabadell)
Installations: Grupo JG
Lighting: Maurici Ginés-Artec
Contractor: G56 / D2S

LOCATION

HISTORICAL PHOTOS. THE 1960s

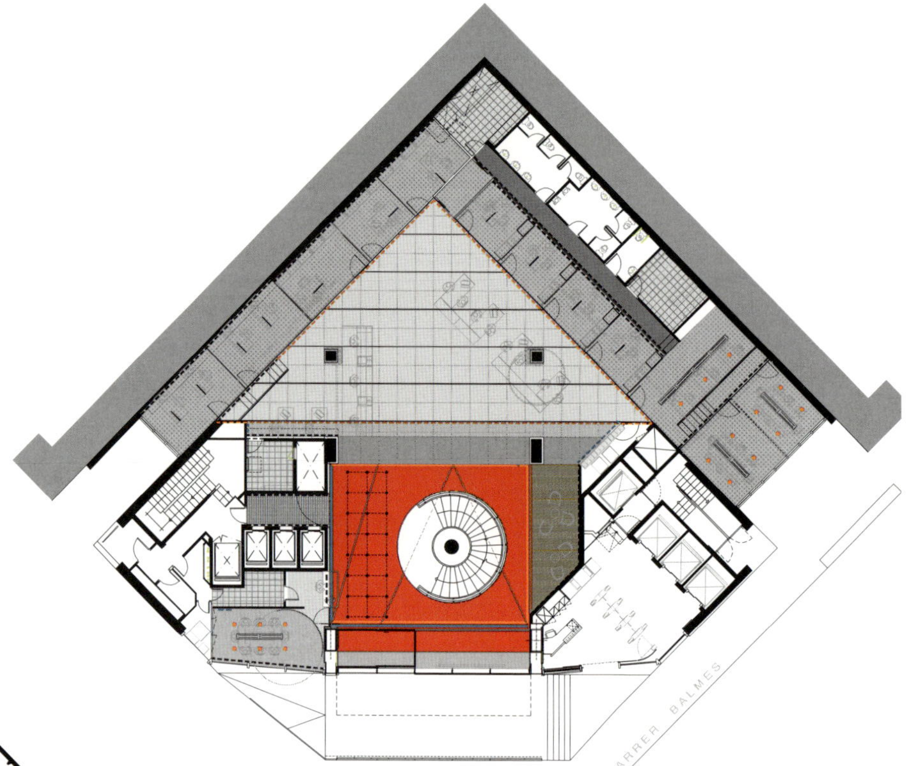

FLOOR PLAN OF FALSE CEILING

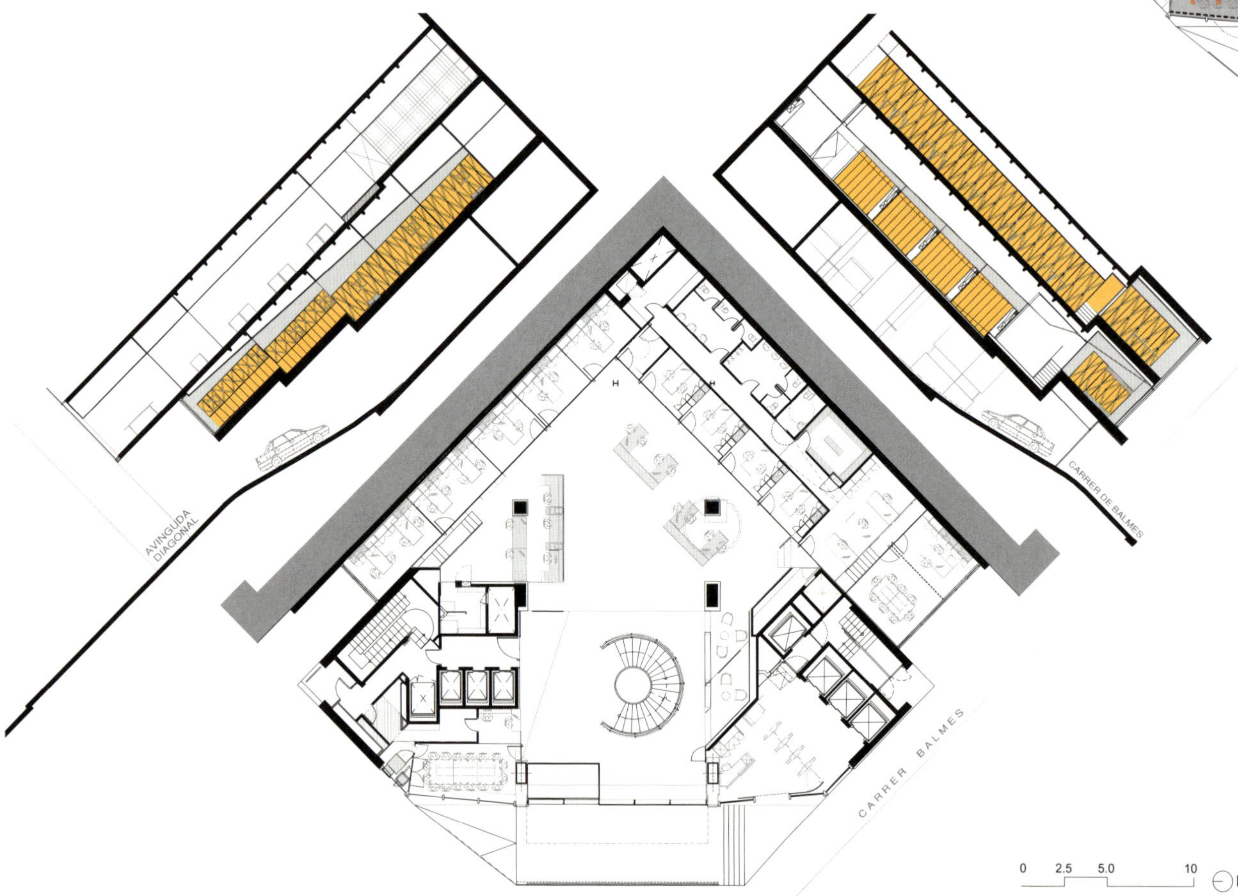

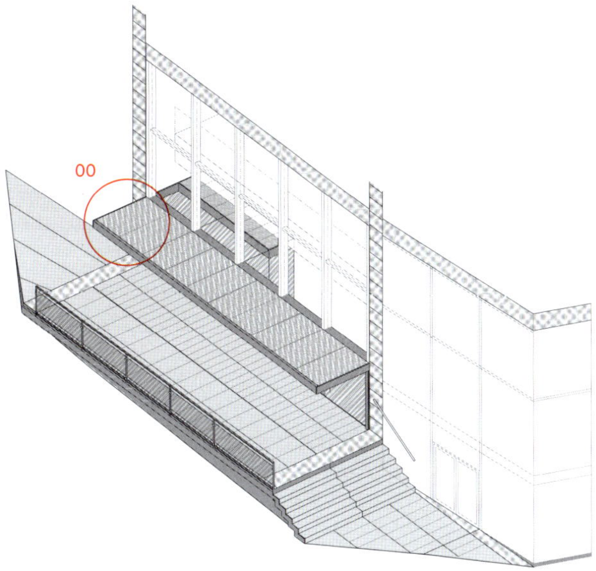

AXONOMETRIC PROJECTION

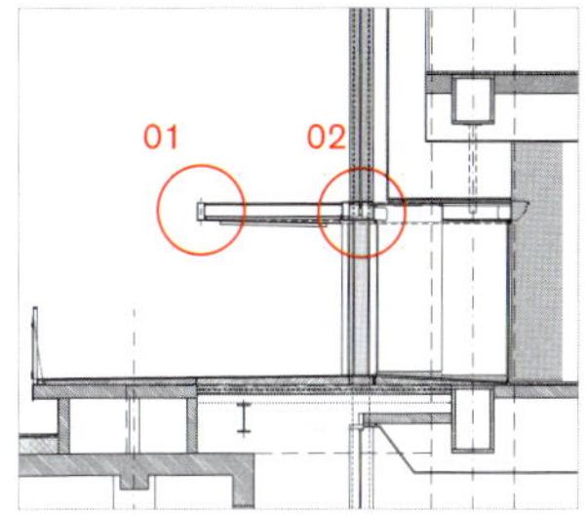

CROSS SECTION

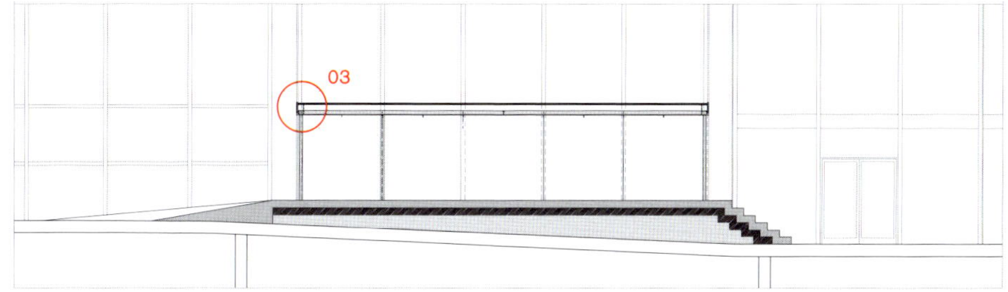

LONGITUDINAL SECTION

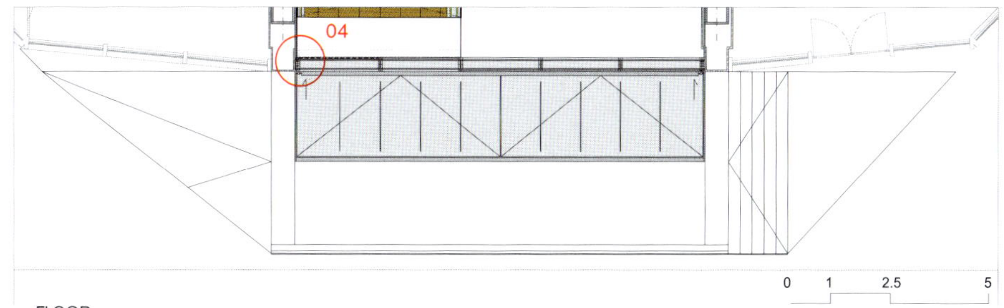

FLOOR

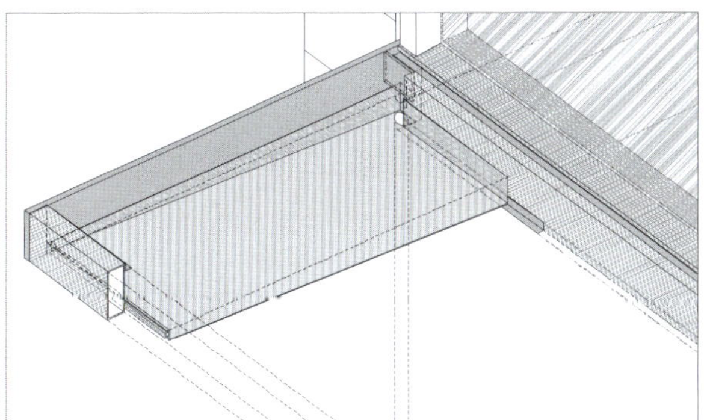

DETAIL 00

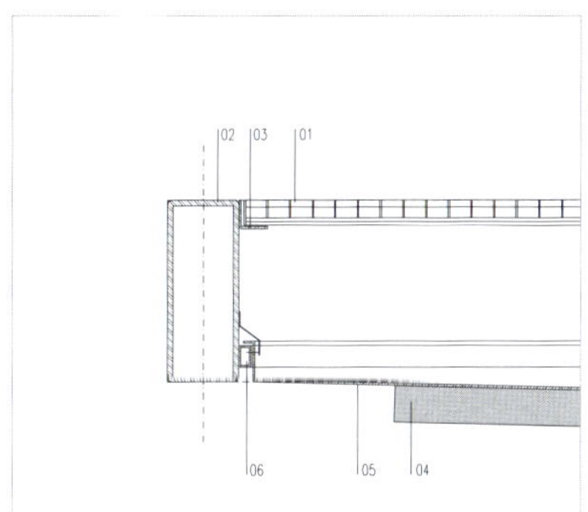

DETAIL 01

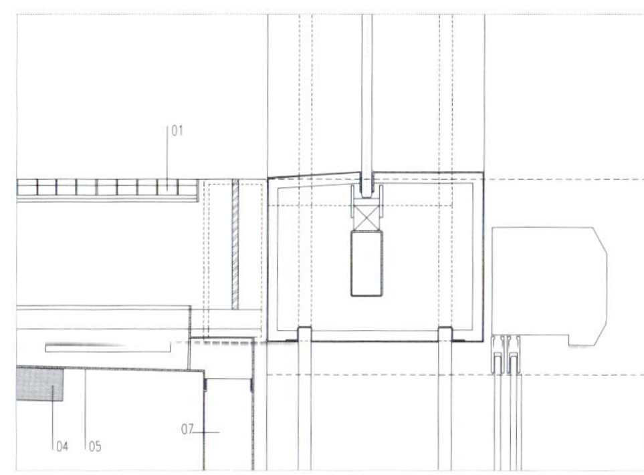

DETAIL 02

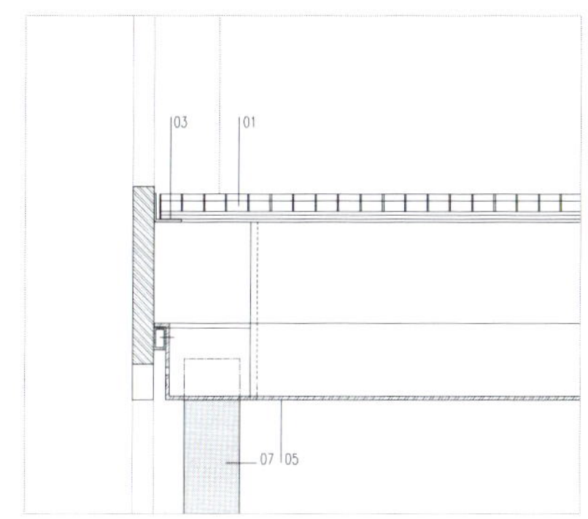

DETAIL 03

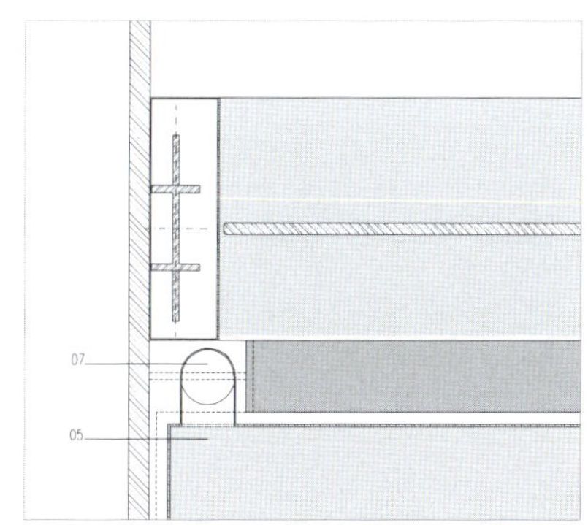

DETAIL 04

MAIN ENTRANCE, AWNING AS GUTTERING TO COLLECT RUN OFF

0 0.25 0.5

Location: La Vall de Bianya, Girona

Surface: 500 m²

External collaborators

Contractor: Puig Alder

LOCATION

PREVIOUS STATE

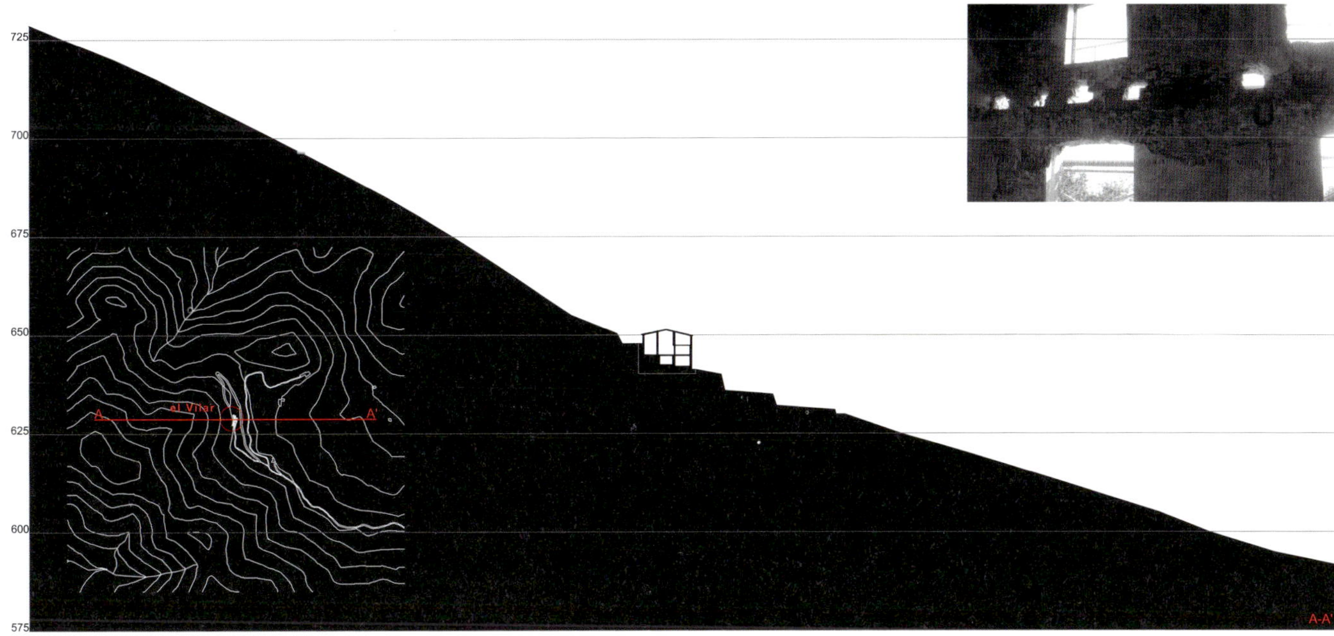

SITE: FLOOR PLAN AND SECTION

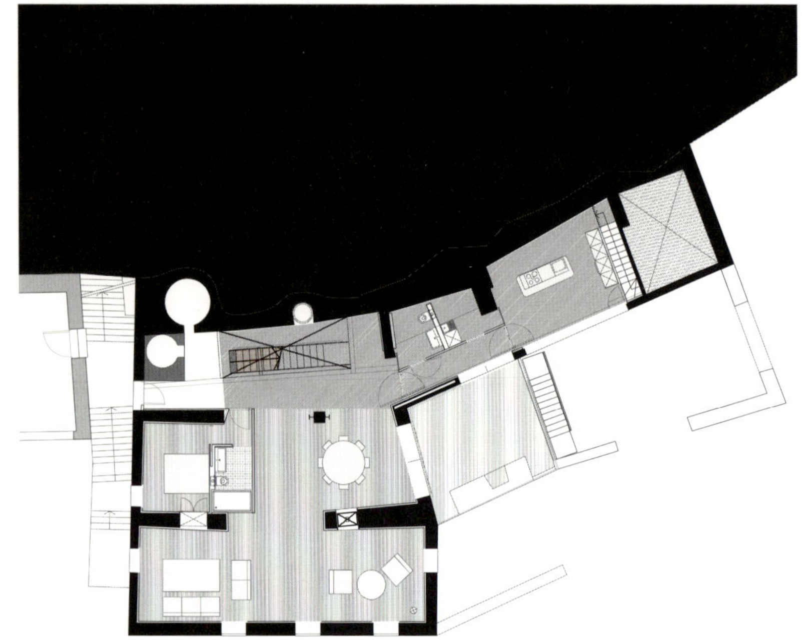

GROUND FLOOR

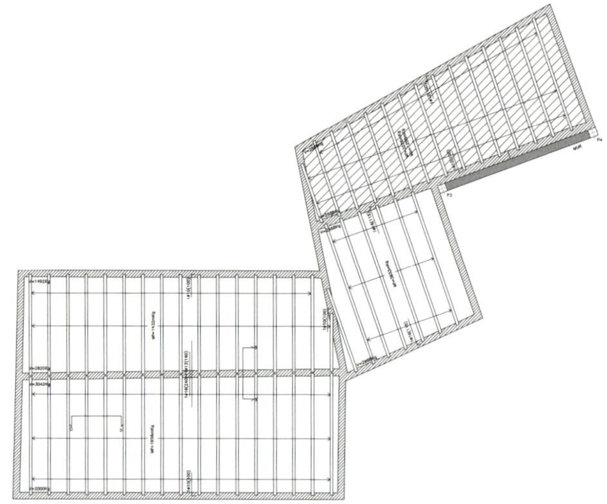

STRUCTURE
CEILING OF BASEMENT FLOOR

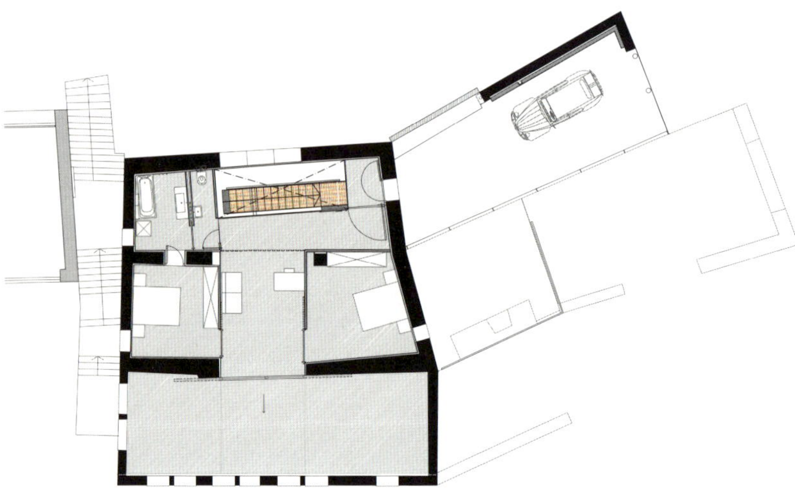

FIRST FLOOR

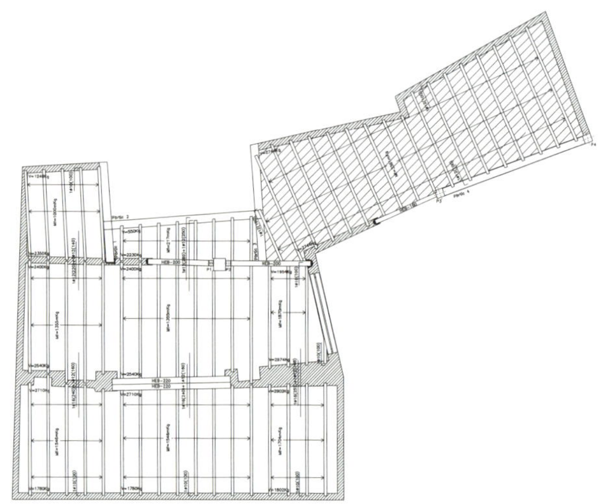

STRUCTURE
CEILING OF GROUND FLOOR

0 2.5 5.0 10 N

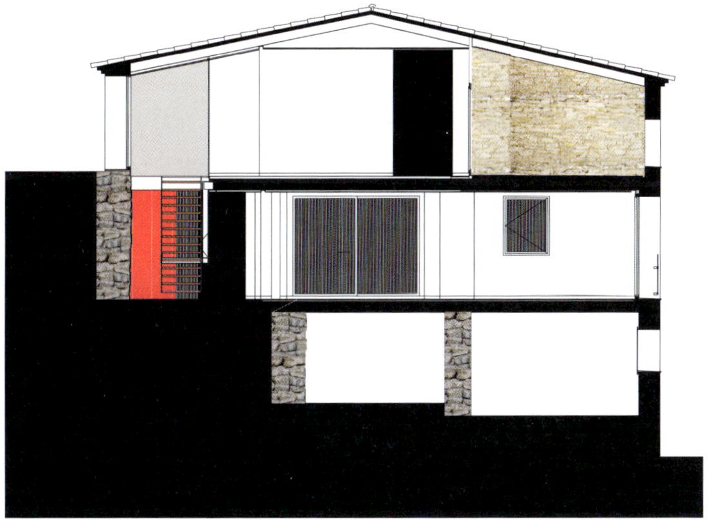

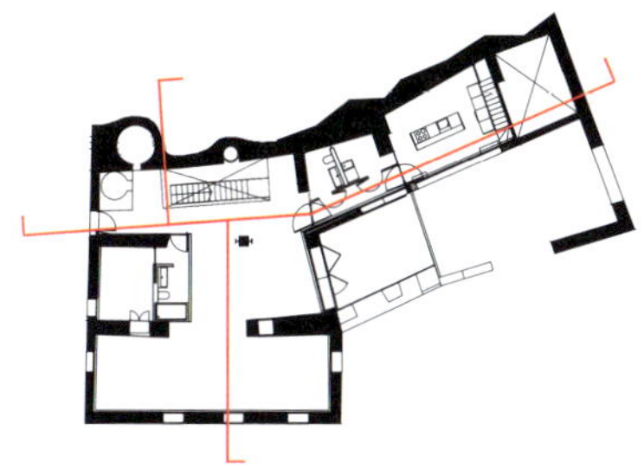

CROSS SECTION

LONGITUDINAL SECTION

0 1 2.5 5

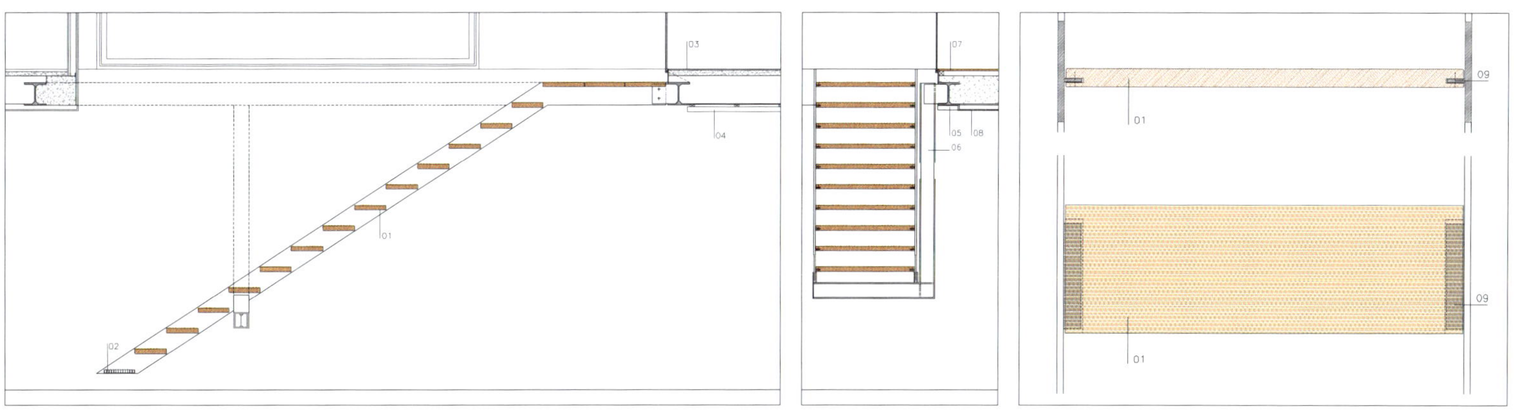

LEGEND
01. 40 mm solid oak steps
02. Galvanised steel step
03. Mat
04. 40 mm black cork
05. 80 x 40 x 5 mm tube
06. 1 bean 140+20 mm plate
07. wood floor
08. plasterboard ceiling
09. 40 x 8 mm crown

DETAILS OF SUSPENDED STAIRWAY

0 0.25 0.5 0.75

First Prize. Invited competition

2004-2011. Barcelona

Location: Plaça Salvador Seguí, Barcelona

Surface: 7,515 m^2

Client: ICIC (Institut Català de les Indústries Culturals)

External collaborators

Structures: BOMA, Agustí Obiol

Installations: Grupo JG

Technical architect: Auding

Budget: Tram

Fire protection: Francesc Labastida

Contractor: Emcofa

LOCATION

Process

Constructing a building can be a long process. This is one of those cases.

1. INVITED COMPETITION. PRESELECTION. SUMMER 2004

The first step was to produce some brief reflections. On the basis of these, plus curriculum and similar documents, the Jury selected five teams.

My initial interest was in understanding the brief and the place. We built a model with fragments of what was to go inside, with no specific attempt to give form or unity. We arranged this conglomerate at a tangent to one of the sides of the site, constructing a street and freeing up a plaza in front of it.

2. RESTRICTED COMPETITION. AUTUMN 2004

The next phase (invitation competition) obviously required precision. The cinemas, a very important part of the project, were put in the basement to reduce the volumetric impact of the building.

The context then became stronger: the plaza became the entire ground floor, and the material for its construction had to be concrete, uniting structure and finish in a continuous mass which, to me, seemed to establish a relation with the shabby, dilapidated masses of its neighbours.

I was particularly interested in the volumetric expressivity of the short sides of the parallelepiped, and its potential to define the corners of the existing streets.

We started talking to the engineers in order to define this open structure at the base (free of pillars, like Lina Bo Bardi's Museum of Art in São Paulo).

We built many models. My drawing, "Gos" (dog in Catalan), synthesised the façades.

3. CONSTRUCTION. 2007-2011

The construction process is extremely complex, having started with a long archaeological dig and continuing with all the excavation and work involved in undergrounding the cinemas, a difficult task because the site is set in a former medieval lagoon. We follow them closely and try to make the process help us: we are trying to convince our client that the archaeological remains should be exhibited, and researching the formal possibilities of the necessary water-resistant concrete.

A building is always the expression of intelligence and a sustained will, brought to bear on a specific place. We cannot abandon the project to its fate. We have to accompany it until the idea, converted into matter and space, starts living its own life. Then, we disappear; the building no longer belongs to us.

Josep Lluís Mateo

1. COMPETITION MODEL (PHASE 1)

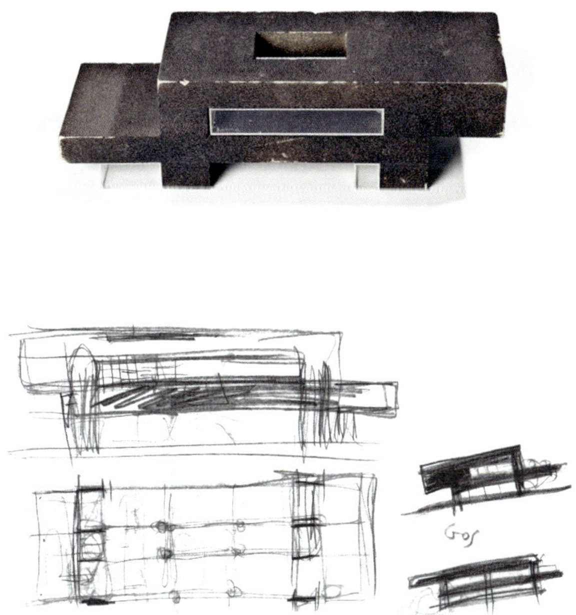

2. COMPETITION MODEL (PHASE 2) AND INITIAL SKETCH

3. FINDING OF ARCHAEOLOGICAL REMAINS AND EXCAVATIONS, 2006

The structure

The building for the Film Theatre of Catalonia, situated in the Barcelona neighbourhood of El Raval, was addressed by means of an absolutely Cartesian geometric layout, made up of two volumes placed one next to the other, with slightly trapezoidal floor plans. One is laid out below grade and therefore finishes at street level; the other rises upwards, confined by its two side façades, whereas the end walls fold in on themselves, giving rise to a succession of projecting volumes.

The functional requirements and the spatial conception of the building rule out the use of intermediate supports in the case of the underground volume, where the screening rooms are housed, as this would compromise the necessary height on some levels, affecting their functional requirements and the transparency that the design deliberately creates throughout the level. Conversely, these conditioning factors do not apply on the underground floors that house secondary uses.

The forcefulness of the chosen geometry practically precludes recourse to structural options that do not turn around the three strong diaphragmatic planes thereby created: the two lengthwise walls that limit the overall volume on these sides, and the dividing wall between the two volumes that go to make it up. The parts of these walls situated below grade are given an absolutely conventional treatment, their singularity being to meet the constructive requirements imposed by the need to form a hermetic space below the water table (it is important to remember that the two outer faces are retaining walls). The walls that extend upwards are "sculpted" in keeping with the demands made by the spaces that they accommodate.

After the primary structure made up of these walls, the secondary structure is extremely simple, comprising systems of parallel beams that were specified as pre-stressed in order to optimize their thickness, which support absolutely conventional floor slabs, in solid slab form. The only singularity of these much smaller floor slabs is found in the ceiling of the screening rooms where, due to their considerable height and to avoid the need for centring, prefabricated slabs were used.

In the high-rise volume, the architecture project included the creation of some completely open-plan floors, specifically the ground and second floors. For this reason, although conceptually the solution used is as explained above, comprising prestressed deep beams and solid slabs, these beams were only actually implemented in the ceilings of floors one and three. As well as supporting the floor slabs corresponding to these ceilings, they also support those

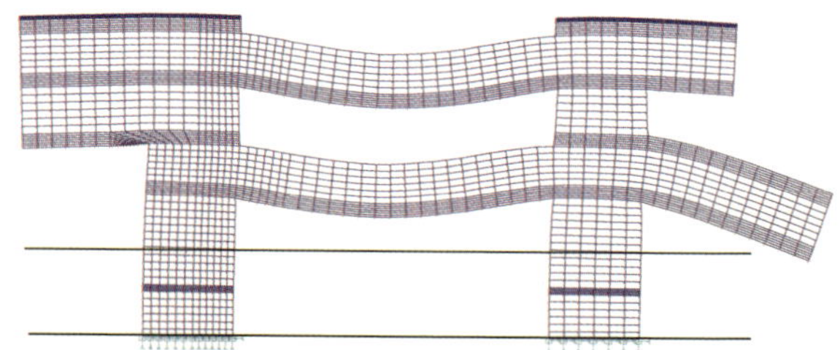

STRUCTURAL DIAGRAM. DEFORMED

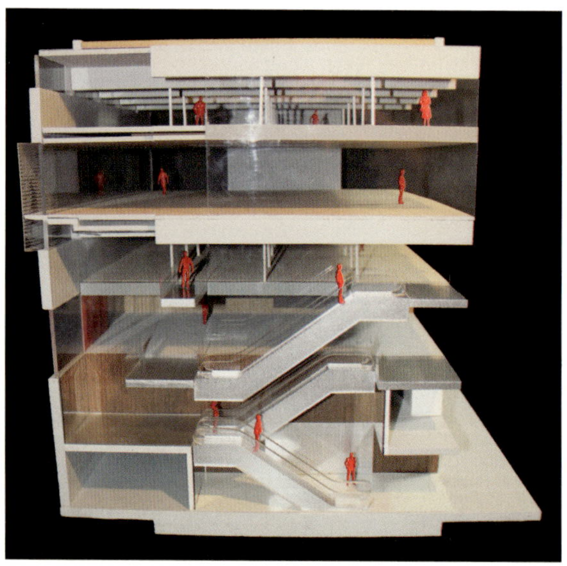

CROSS SECTION MODEL

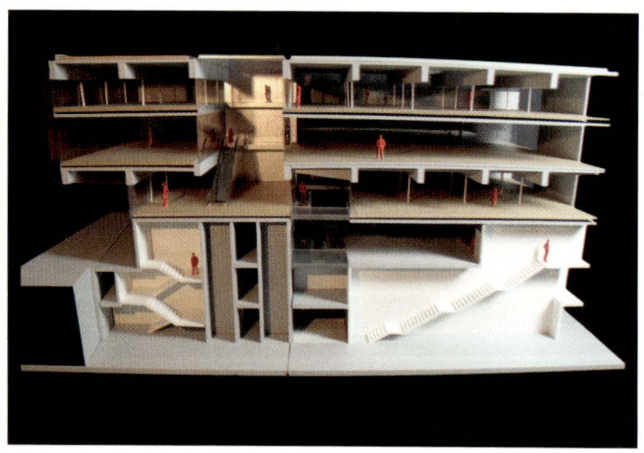

LONGITUDINAL SECTION MODEL

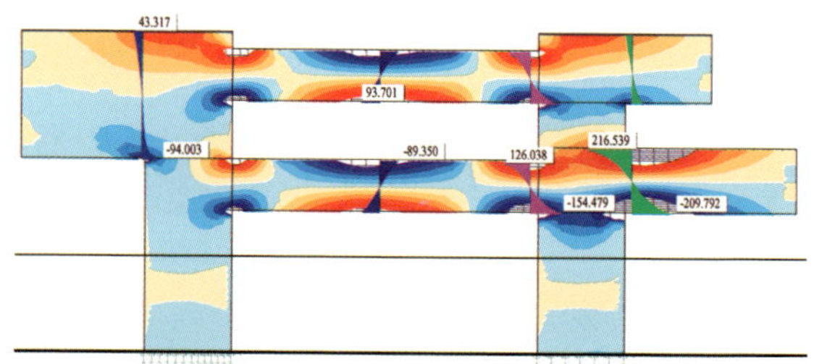

STRUCTURAL DIAGRAM. TENSIONS Y-Y

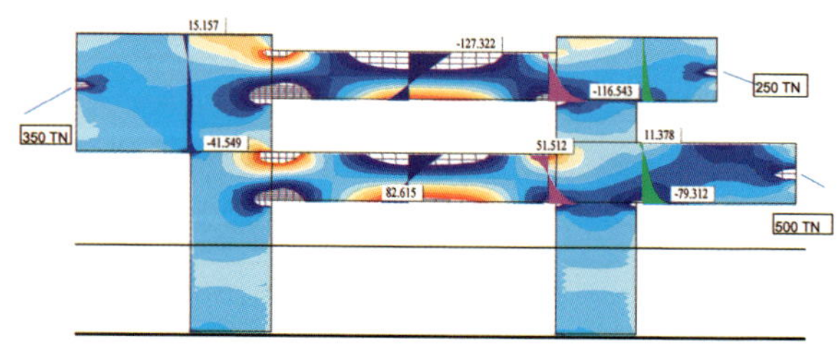

STRUCTURAL DIAGRAM. TENSIONS Y-Y, POST-TENSIONING

of the corresponding floors, thanks to a perfectly ordered arrangement of ties that suspend them from the floor beams.

The most singular elements in this structural framework are probably the two side walls (longitudinal façade) of the high-rise volume. These walls present an extensive surface perforated by openings, many of them very large and extending beyond their constrained areas of support to form large projections to either side.

For this reason, they were actually designed and constructed as two large pre-stressed beams, with systems of curvilinear tension at varying levels generating geometries which, as is habitual in this technique, follow almost mimetically the lines of the diagrams of bending moments in the system. The trajectories of these tendons become "transparent" in the façade walls, taking the form of discontinuous recesses that reveal their positions.

Agustí Obiol

HEADS OF THE POST-TENSIONED BEAMS IN THE FAÇADE

POSITION OF THE TENDONS IN THE FAÇADE

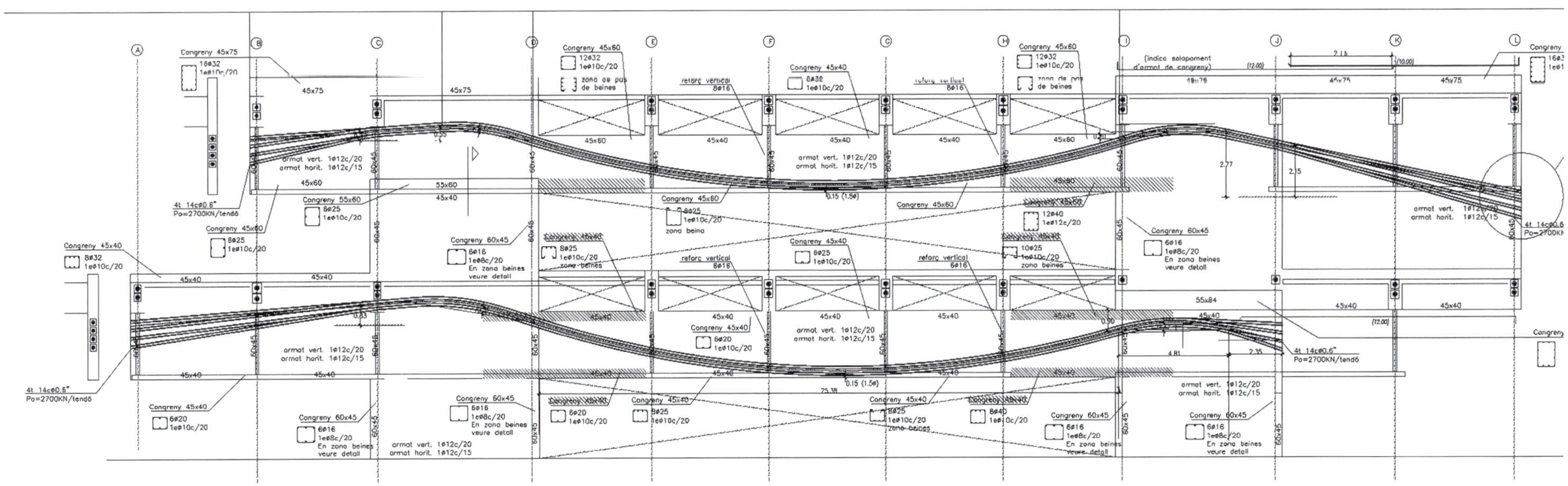

STRUCTURAL ELEVATION OF THE WALL

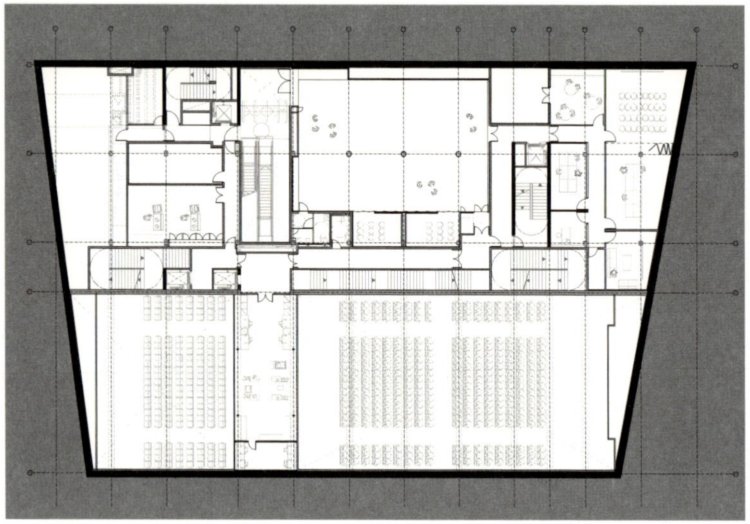

BASEMENT 1 FLOOR PLAN

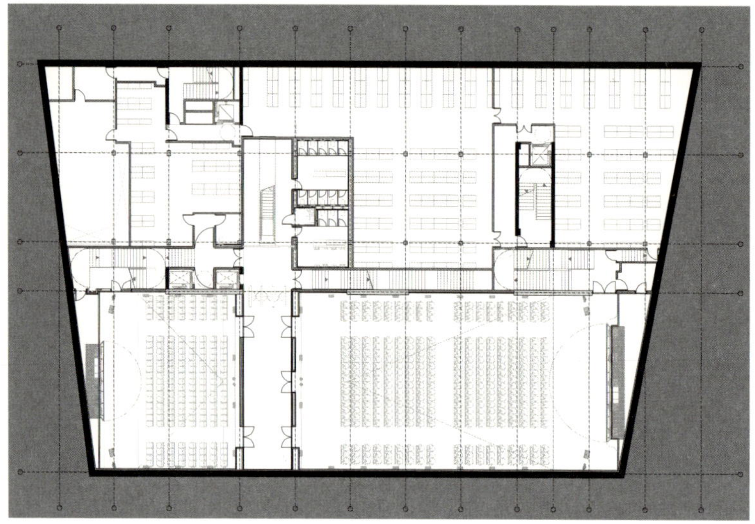

BASEMENT 2 FLOOR PLAN

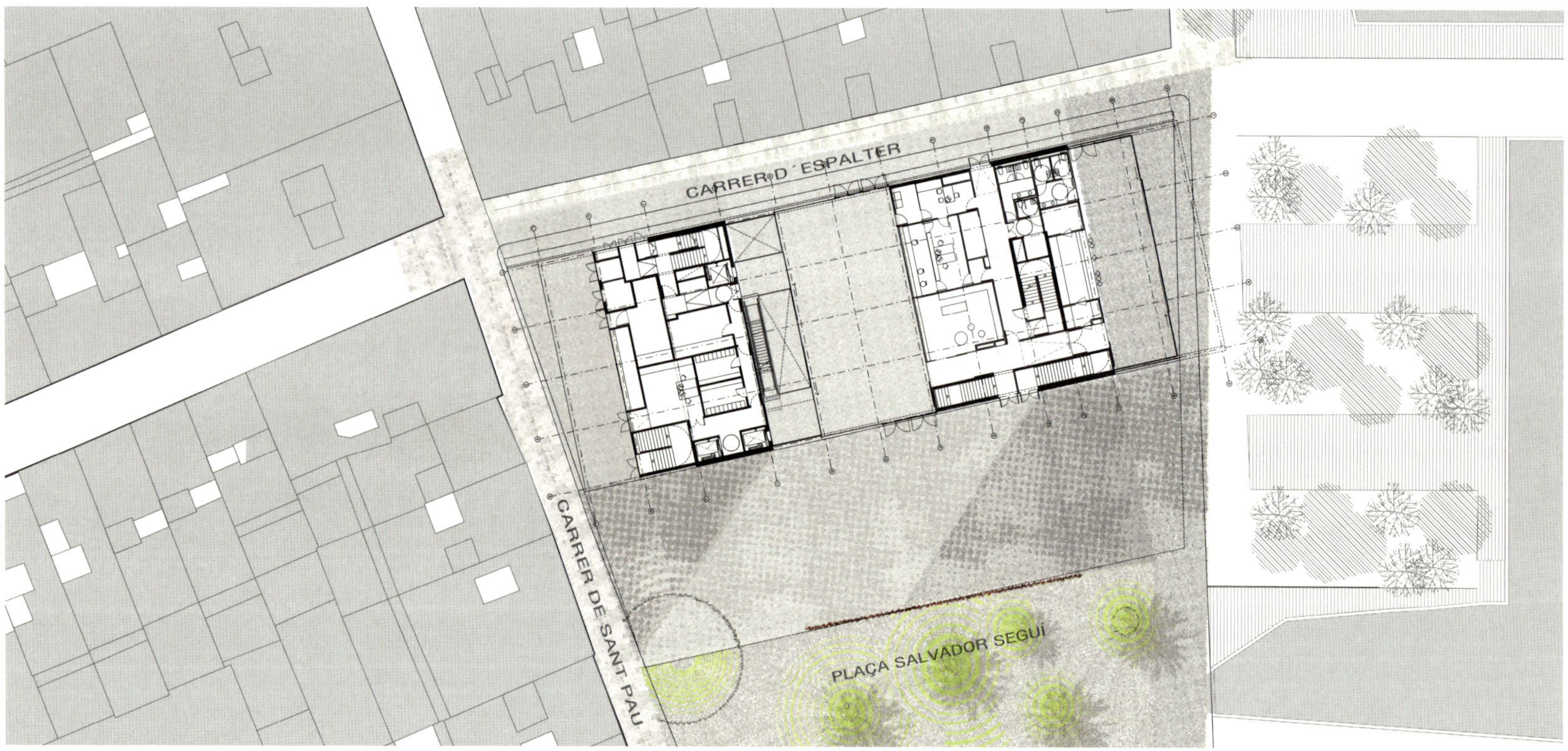

GROUND FLOOR PLAN

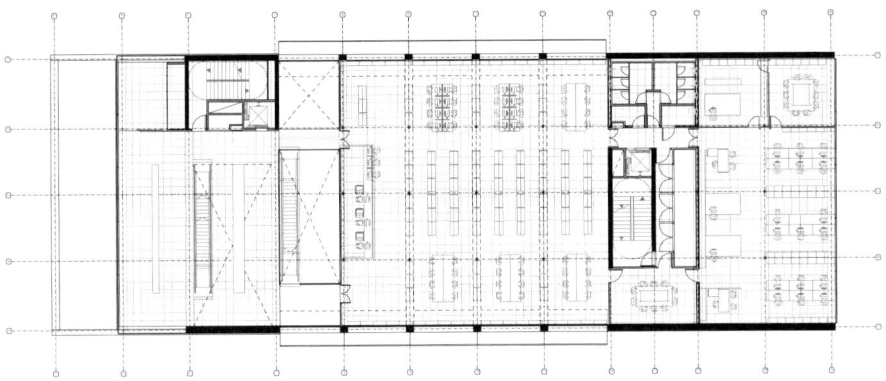

FIRST FLOOR PLAN

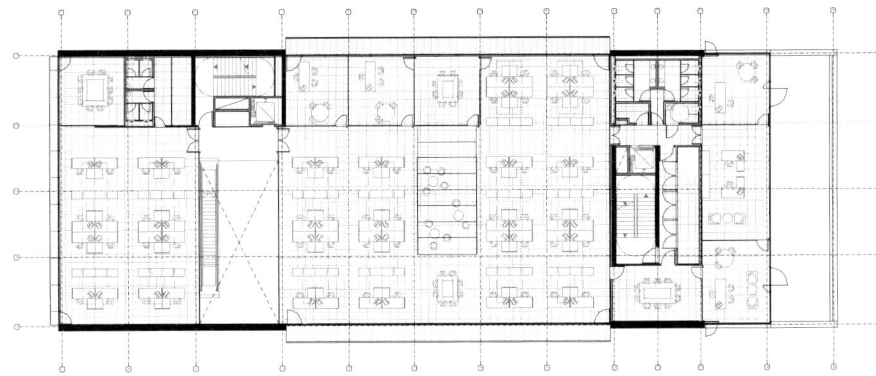

SECOND FLOOR PLAN

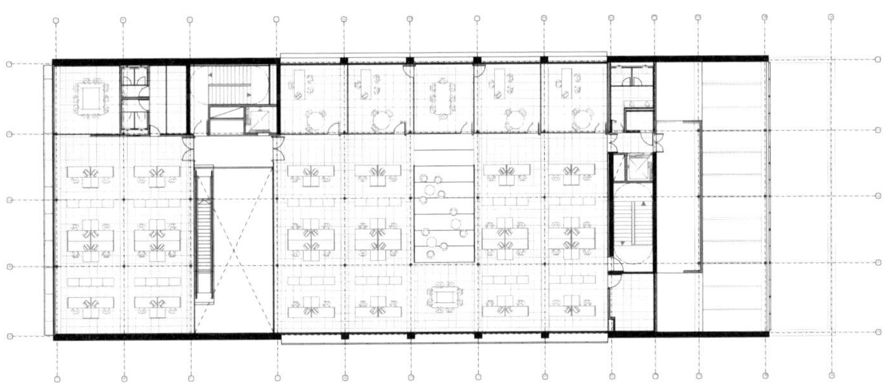

THIRD FLOOR PLAN

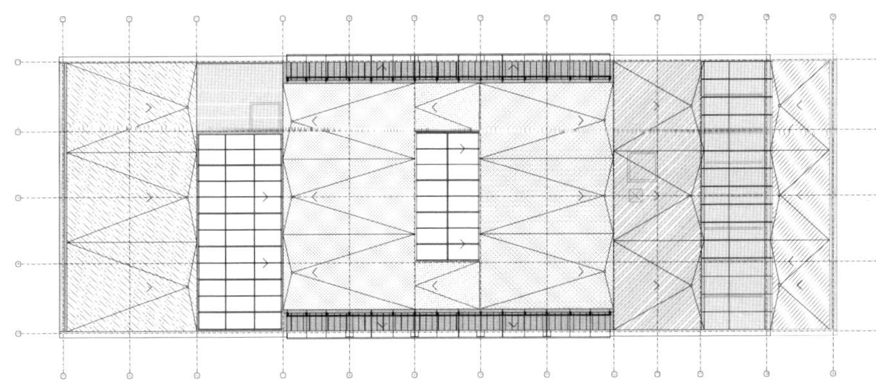

ROOF PLAN

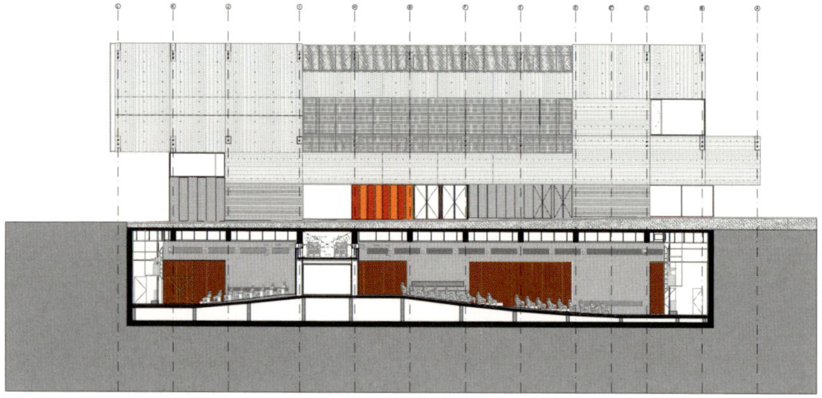

SECTION 01

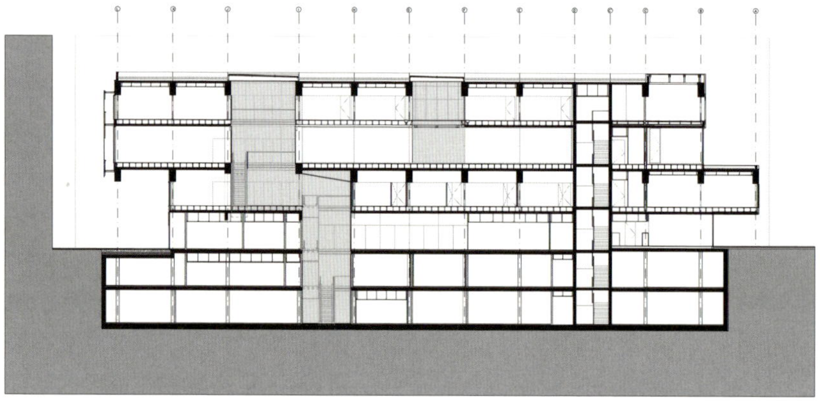

SECTION 02

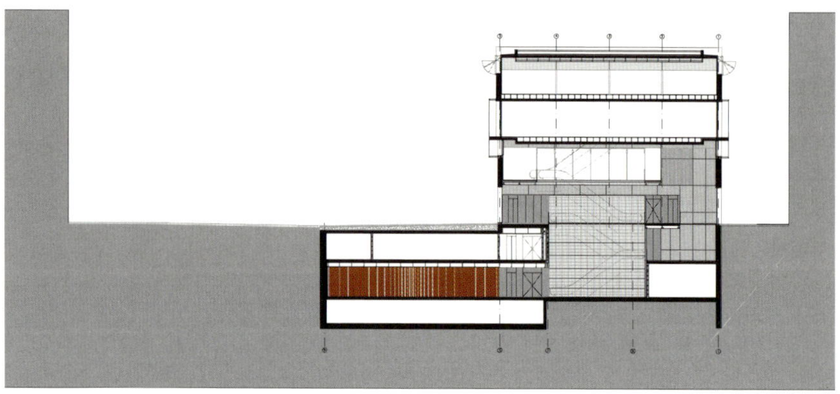

SECTION 03

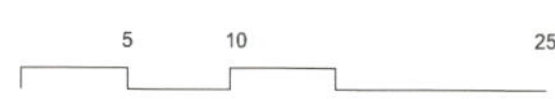

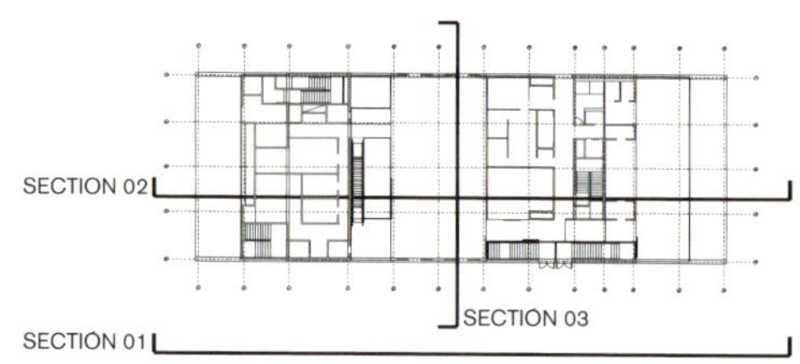

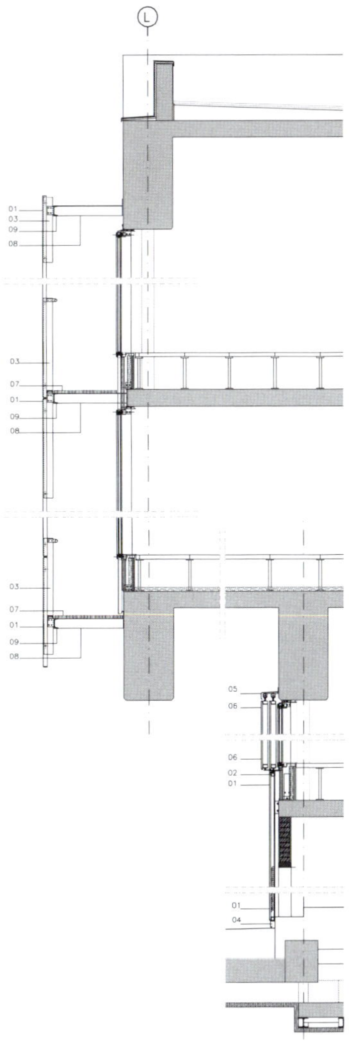

section 01_FAÇADE C/ ST. PAU_COR-TEN

01_folded Cor-ten steel sheet panels, 3 mm (06_sliding)
03_supporting structure, painted galvanized steel plate, 110 x 2 mm
04_05_finish top and bottom of folded Cor-ten steel sheet, 3 mm
07_galvanized steel grid with 25 x 25 mm spacing and 20 x 2 mm plates
08_structural T with 120 mm flange every 927 mm
09_American standard channel, 120 mm

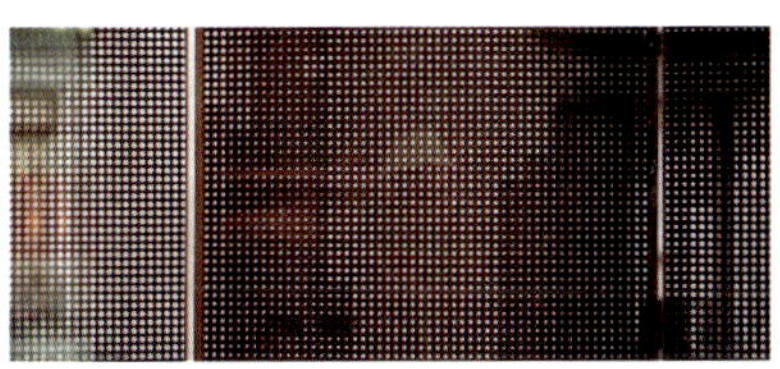

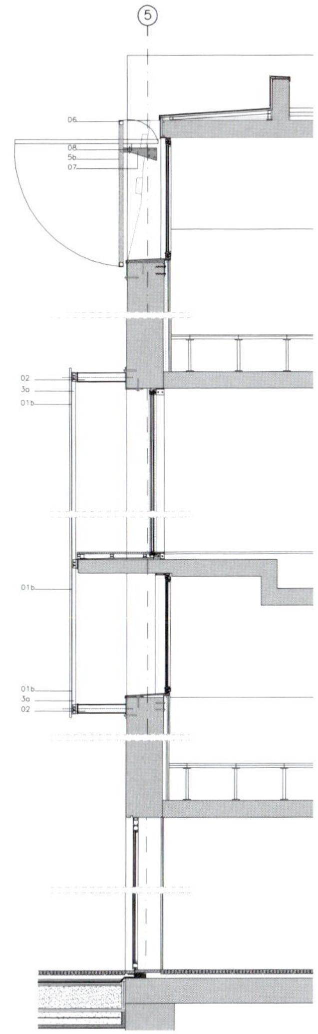

section 02_FAÇADE PLAÇA SALVADOR SEGUÍ_MESH

01b_white stainless steel mesh, variable density
Awnings:
02_supporting structure, galvanized steel tube, 50 x 25 x 2 mm
03_supporting structure: painted galvanized steel
3a. T50 mm bars, attached by screws to a double plate
3b. 50 x 20 mm and 50 x 25 mm tubes (at the ends) attached to T bars
05_Fabric awning in gold (a) white (b)
06_50 x 50 mm tube
07_10 mm plate attached with 15 mm spacers
08_tube with motor incorporated inside

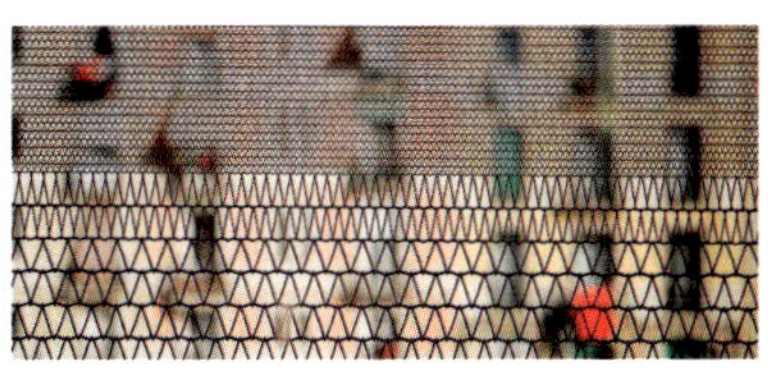

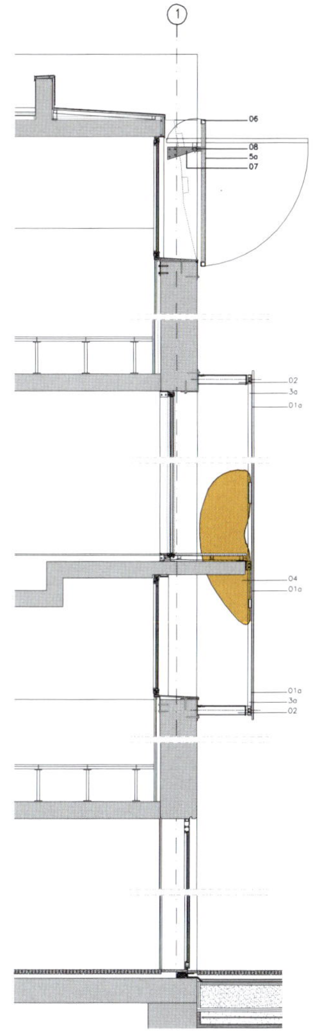

section 03_FAÇADE C/ ESPALTER_EXPANDED

01a_2 mm galvanized steel sheet, perforated and expanded, powder coated and riveted to vertical tubes
02_main structure: 114 mm tubular sections and 120 x 10 mm continuous plate of black-painted hot galvanized steel
03_supporting structure: painted galvanized steel
3a. T50 mm bars, attached by screws to a double plate
3b. 50 x 20 mm and 50 x 25 mm tubes (at the ends) attached to T bars
04_side railing: painted steel sheet
05_Fabric awning in gold (a) white (b)
07_10 mm plate attached with 15 mm spacers
08_tube with motor incorporated inside

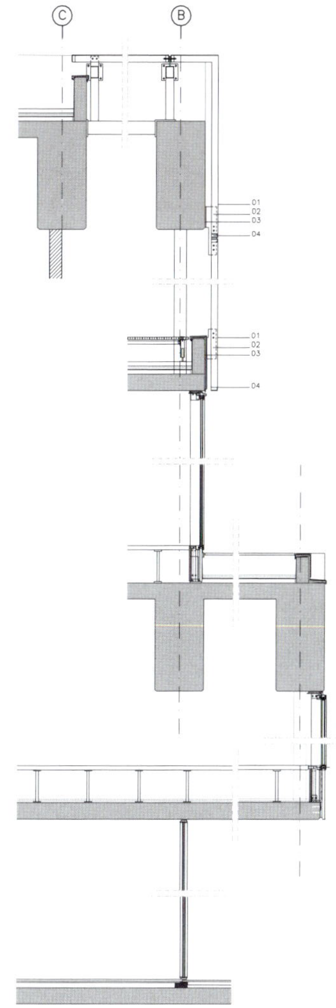

section 04_FAÇADE C/ST. JOSEP ORIOL_METAL GRID

01_galvanized steel grid with 25 x 25 mm spacing and 20 x 2 mm plates
02_supporting structure, painted galvanized steel plate, 600 x 10 x 2 mm
03_steel sheet anchored to the concrete structure with mechanical bolts
04_perimeter structure of galvanized steel tube, 80 x 40 mm

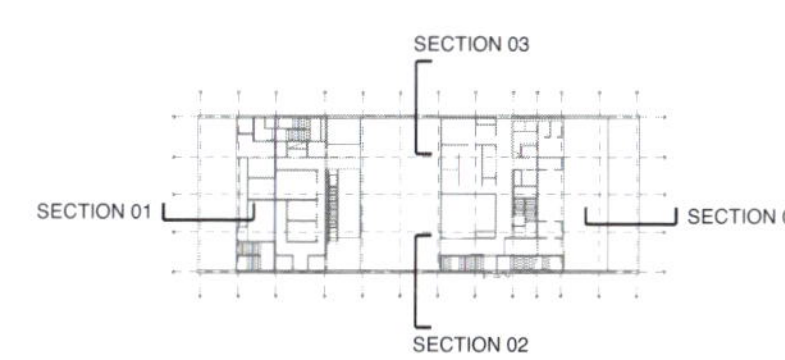

Josep Lluís Mateo
Architect since 1974 and PhD (*cum laude*) since 1994 at the UPC-Universitat Politècnica de Catalunya. He is Professor of Architecture and Projects at the ETH-Eidgenössische Technische Hochschule (Swiss Federal Polytechnic).
In addition to the works presented in this book, landmarks in his career as an architect, for which he was recently awarded the A+ Prize 2011, include the development of Ullastret (Santander Biennale Prize 1991), housing on Borneo Island in Amsterdam (CEOE Prize 2001), the head office of the Bundesbank in Chemnitz (2004), the Forum 2004 complex in Barcelona, the Barcelona International Convention Centre (CCIB), Hotel AC and the CZF office block, the Sant Jordi student residence (Archizinc Prize 2008) and the WTC Almeda Park office building in Cornellà (A+ Prize for Work Architecture 2010).
His work has been extensively published and exhibited, most recently at the MoMA (New York, 2006), the Pavillon de l'Arsénal (Paris, 2009), the Glyptotheque (Athens, 2010) and the Central House of Artists (Moscow, 2011).

Agustí Obiol Sánchez
Agustí Obiol is an architect (Universitat Politècnica de Catalunya-UPC, 1975) and PhD in Architecture (1977), and was awarded the ETSAB's extraordinary prize for the best doctoral thesis. He was assistant lecturer in Structures I and II in 1979 and has been Professor of Structures II since 1981. He currently teaches at the Barcelona School of Architecture.
He is a member of the Board of Directors and Head of Energy & Building Technologies at the Barcelona Institute of Architecture, and is a member of the Col·legi Oficial d'Arquitectes de Catalunya (COAC), the International Centre for Numerical Methods in Engineering and the Associació de Consultors d'Estructures de Catalunya.
In his professional field, he was founder member of BOMA structural consultancy in 1979, and has designed the structures of dozens of buildings by renowned architects, such as the Olympic Pavilion in Badalona, Hotel Arts, AGBAR Tower, Hotel Hesperia Tower, the Barcelona International Convention Centre, the Americas Cup Foredeck building in Valencia and the rehabilitation of the Museu Nacional d'Art de Catalunya.

Dominique Boudet
Dominique Boudet is an architecture journalist and critic, and was editorial director and editor-in-chief of *AMC* magazine. He was involved in creating the Prix Equerre d'Argent and the Prix de la Première œuvre, now recognised as France's top architecture prizes. In 2000, he set up the European Architects' Forum to offer the new generation of European architects a place to debate questions of common interest. He is a contributor to various European architecture magazines (*de Architect* in Holland and *Architektur Aktuell* in Austria) and participates on international teams, offering consultations on large-scale urban projects in cities such as Nice, Bordeaux and Toulouse. He was curator of the exhibition "Double or Nothing", the first retrospective of Belgian architecture practice 51N4E (Palais des Beaux-arts, Brussels, 2011) and is currently working on a monograph about the French architects Jean-Marc Ibos and Myrto Vitart.

Philip Ursprung
Philip Ursprung studied Art History, History and German literature in Geneva, Vienna and Berlin, receiving his PhD from the Freie Universität Berlin. He has taught at the University of Geneva, at the ETH Zurich and at the Hochschule der Künste Berlin. In 2007, he was visiting professor at the Graduate School of Architecture, Planning and Preservation of Columbia University, New York.
From 2005 to 2010, he was professor of Modern and Contemporary Art at the University of Zurich. He was a visiting curator at the Canadian Centre for Architecture in Montreal where he curated "Herzog & de Meuron: Archeology of the Mind" and edited the catalogue *Herzog & de Meuron: Natural History* (2002). His publications include *Grenzen der Kunst: Allan Kaprow und das Happening* and *Robert Smithson und die Land Art* (Munich: Silke Schreiber, 2003). He contributed to the introduction of *Studio Olafur Eliasson: An Encyclopedia* (Cologne: Taschen, 2008) and is the editor of *Caruso St John: Almost Everything* (Barcelona: Polígrafa, 2008). His most recent book is *Kunst der Gegenwart: 1960 bis heute* (Munich: Beck, 2010).

Fredy Massad and Alicia Guerrero Yeste
Fredy Massad is an architect and critic. He studied architecture at the University of Buenos Aires, where he is currently assistant lecturer in the Soloona Lodooma-Salama Chair. Alicia Guerrero Yeste has a degree in Art History from the University of Lleida. Together they set up ¿btbW/ Architecture in 1996, devoting their joint practice to research and analysis of contemporary architecture. They currently work as critics for *EXIT Express* magazine and the cultural supplements of *ABC* and *La Vanguardia*, and contribute to various international media specializing in architecture and design. They also teach at Elisava-Barcelona Graduate Design School (Universitat Pompeu Fabra).
At international level, they lecture and participate in symposiums at universities, bringing a critical approach to the fundamental situations defining the present state of architecture. They are the authors of *Notas sobre ciudades (mutantes)* (1998) and *Enric Miralles. Metamorfosi del Paesaggio* (2004), and editors of *a+a architecturanimation* (2002), the "Arquitectura en la era de la revolución digital" monographic for *Experimenta* magazine (2003) and *ExpoZaragoza: Un proyecto urbano* (2008).

Adrià Goula Sardà
Adrià Goula studied at the Barcelona School of Architecture, qualifying as an architect in 2000 and gaining a Diploma in Advanced Studies in 2007. He works as an architect with various practices in Barcelona and Paris, and in 2005 he set up his own studio, aH! Arquitectura, combining architectural practice and photography, which is now his principal activity. In this field, he works with well-known local and international architects, and various public and private institutions. His work has been published in numerous magazines such as *AV*, *Quaderns*, *Frame*, *AMC* and *Detail*, and in several monographic books. In 2010 and 2011 he taught the Architectural Photography course at the Sert School, and has been invited to talk about his work in a variety of courses and workshops. As a freelance photographer, he addresses other themes and has had one-man shows in Paris, Bordeaux and Barcelona. In 2009, Fundación Esteyco published his book *De-Construcción*.

MATEO ARQUITECTURA
Management:
Josep Lluís Mateo
Marta Cervelló (associate architect)

Project leaders:
Anna Llimona. Architect, ETSA Barcelona
Laurent Baudelot. Architecte diplômé par le Gouvernement, École d'Architecture de Paris-Belleville (France)
Till von Mackensen. Diplom-Ingenieur (Architektur), Technische Universität Darmstadt (Germany)
Xavier Monclús. Technical architect, EUP Barcelona

Team (2009-2011) :
Vicky Daroca, Marta Poch, Victor Molina, Enric Sanitjas, Anabel Linares, Marc Pi, Coraline Govers, Rabindranath Andujar, Marco Podestá, Marta González, Patricia Baztán, Eloi Coloma, Oia Pursals, Anna Profitós, Marina Montori, Cecilia Tobler, Marta Gual, María Martínez, José García, James Yeo, Aida Mejía, Eduard Balcells, Miriam Roure, Joanna Ejsmont, Èlia Canadell, Blanca Lora-Tamayo, Frédéric Géraud

Administration:
Isabel Riambau
Salvador Torroja

Communication:
Maria Matamala
Keymedia SL

Information systems:
Eupalinos-Cooperativa d'Arquitectes Jordi Capell

www.mateo-arquitectura.com

Photographs:
Adrià Goula Photo: Adrià Goula (Photographs), Xavi Alias (Postproduction), Maria Elisa Ojeda (Communication)
www.adriagoula.com

OFFICES IN BOULOGNE-BILLANCOURT. FRANCE 2010
First prize. Invited competition. 3 phases
2006-2010. Paris/France
Location: Rue Émile Zola, Boulogne-Billancourt, Paris
Surface area: 15,500 m²
Client: VINCI Immobilier d'entreprise / NEXITY Entreprises
Team:
Competition with: Agence SAISON-MENU architecture: Isabelle Menu, Annabelle Vérecque
Competition bid leader: Vicky Daroca
Project leader: Laurent Baudelot
Project team: Johan Cordonnier, Pedro Duarte, Sabrina Németh, Till Von Mackensen, Pascal Babey, François Jaubert, Marianne Baumgartner, Joana Ramalhete
Site management: Laurent Baudelot with Xavier Monclús and Anna Llimona
External collaborators:
Structure and installations: SNC Lavalin / Agustí Obiol-BOMA
Quality control: VERITAS
Fire protection: EURO Coord
Energy control: COTEBA Environnement
Acoustics: Lasa
Landscaping: D'ici-là
Façades: Interface
Contractor: Sicra

PGGM COMPANY HEADQUARTERS. ZEIST, HOLLAND 2011
First prize. Invited competition
2002-2011. Zeist/Holland
Location: Noordweg Noord, Zeist
Surface area: 25,000 m² offices, 25,000 m² parking spaces
Client: PGGM Insurance Company
Team:
Competition with: Luca Gazzaniga
Competition bid leader: Markus Lauber
Competition team: Héctor Mendoza, Pilar Ferreres, Marta Poch, Michel Rocchach
Project leader: Coraline Govers, Mathijs van Daal, Markus Lauber, Till von Mackensen
Project team: Xavier Monclús, Héctor Mendoza, Boris Bezan, Nataly Wierenga, Enriqueta Llabrés, Arnoud Hulpia, Cristina Fernández, Emile van Vugt, Johan Cordonnier
Site management: Victoria Llinares, Coraline Govers, Till von Mackensen, Enriqueta Labrés, Xavier Monclús
External collaborators:
Structures: Zonnefeld
Installations: Deerns
Physics: Peutz
Landscaping: Deltavorm
Local architect: ADP-Marc a Campo
Coordinator: Steven de Haas
Project manager: B.B.N.
Contractor: Ballast Nedam

INTERVENTIONS IN BANC SABADELL. BARCELONA 2010
2006-2010. Barcelona
Location: Diagonal with Balmes, Barcelona
Surface area: 1,000 m²
Client: Banc Sabadell
Team:
Project leader: Ismael Heras, Vicky Daroca, Marta González
Project team: Mariana Castro, Sara Cardoso, Miriam Moreno, Xavier Monclús, Oía Pursals
Site management: Ismael Heras, Vicky Daroca, Marta González
External collaborators:
Structure: BOMA
Installations: Grupo JG
Technical architect: Francina Bernad (Banc Sabadell)
Lighting: Maurici Ginés-Artec
Contractor: G56 / D2S

RECONSTRUCTION OF AN OLD RURAL MANSION. LA GARROTXA, GIRONA PROVINCE, 2010
2006-2010. La Vall de Bianya, Girona province
Location: La Vall de Bianya, Girona province
Surface area: 500 m²
Team:
With: Dot Arquitectes (Bet Capdeferro, Ramón Bosch)
Project leader and Site management: Xavier Monclús and Xavier de Bolos
External collaborators:
Contractor: Puig Alder

FILM THEATRE OF CATALONIA. BARCELONA 2011
First prize. Invited competition
2004-2011. Barcelona
Location: Plaça Salvador Seguí, Barcelona
Surface area: 7,515 m²
Client: ICIC (Institut Català de les Indústries Culturals)
Team:
Competition team: Marc Camallonga, Enriqueta Llabrés, Adriana Porta, Lucas Echeveste, Ismael Heras, Daniel Blüm
Project leader: Jordi Pagès
Project team: Xavier Monclús, Enriqueta Llabrés, Benjamin Scharf, Maria Matamala
Site management: Vicky Daroca, Marc Pi, Xavier Monclús, Marta Gual
External collaborators:
Structures: BOMA, Agustí Obiol
Installations: Grupo JG
Technical architect: Auding
Budget: Tram
Fire protection: Francesc Labastida
Acoustics: Higini Arau
Graphic design: Teresa Guix
Contractor: Emcofa

CREDITS

Published by
EDICIONES POLÍGRAFA
Balmes, 54, ent. 2ª
08007 Barcelona
www.edicionespoligrafa.com

Editor
Josep Lluís Mateo

Editorial coordination
Maria Matamala

Texts
Josep Lluís Mateo
Agustí Obiol
Dominique Boudet
Fredy Massad
Alicia Guerrero
Philip Ursprung
Adrià Goula
Lucien Engels

Graphic Design and Digital Production
Actar Pro

Photographs
Adrià Goula

Translation and proofreading
Elaine Fradley

Printing
INGOPRINT S.L.

ISBN: 978-84-343-1312-5
DL: B-9.077-2012

Available in USA and Canada through D.A.P./Distributed
Art Publishers
155 Sixth Avenue, 2nd Floor, New York, N. Y. 10013
Tel. (212) 627-1999 Fax: (212) 627-9484